BEING AN **INFORMATION INNOVATOR**

Jennifer Rowley

facet publishing

Published by Facet Publishing
7 Ridgmount Street, London WC1E 7AE
www.facetpublishing.co.uk

Facet Publishing is wholly owned by CILIP: the Chartered Institute
of Library and Information Professionals.

British Library Cataloguing in Publication Data
A catalogue record for this book is available from the British Library.
ISBN 978-1-85604-671-8

First published 2011
Reprinted digitally thereafter

Mixed Sources
Product group from well-managed
forests and other controlled sources
www.fsc.org Cert no. SA-COC-1565
© 1996 Forest Stewardship Council
FSC

Text printed on FSC accredited material.

Typeset from author's files in 10.5/14.5 pt Dutch 823 and
Humanist 777 by Facet Publishing Production.
Printed and made in Great Britain by MPG Books Group, UK.

BEING AN **INFORMATION INNOVATOR**

By the same author from Facet Publishing:

Sue Roberts and Jennifer Rowley
Managing Information Services
ISBN 978-1-85604-515-5

Sue Roberts and Jennifer Rowley
Leadership: the challenge for the information profession
ISBN 978-1-85604-609-1

Contents

Acknowledgements

First and foremost, I would like to acknowledge the contributions from two colleagues who co-authored two of the chapters. Anahita Baregheh, a PhD researcher in innovation at Bangor Business School, co-authored Chapter 2. Dr Siwan Mitchelmore, Lecturer in Entrepreneurship at Bangor Business School, co-authored Chapter 3.

In addition, I would like to express my thanks to all of the authors who have made diverse contributions to thinking, knowledge and practice in innovation, creativity and entrepreneurship, and who have informed the writing of this book in various ways. I am also grateful to a number of organizations for permission to reproduce extracts from their documents or websites. Acknowledgement is included adjacent to the individual items.

Finally, I would like to express my thanks to the team at Facet Publishing whose enthusiasm and encouragement and, in this case more than usual, patience have been invaluable.

Introduction

While there is no shortage of articles and books discussing the changing nature of libraries in the digital age, words such as 'innovation', 'entrepreneurship', 'entrepreneur', 'intrapreneur' and 'creativity' make only occasional appearances in the information management literature. There are a few key contributions that argue for the link between innovation, entrepreneurship and creativity and change in libraries (Mason, 1989; Riggs, 2001) but without a much wider discussion there is a danger that information professionals and library managers may miss the opportunity to engage in and manage innovation effectively; act entrepreneurially; encourage others to act entrepreneurially; and embrace and develop their creativity.

This book, then, is the first to seek to discuss and apply the rhetoric and theories of innovation and entrepreneurship in information organizations. It seeks both to celebrate and share past achievements and existing examples of good practice in these areas, as well as to provide frameworks and concepts that promote reflection on the development of innovative and entrepreneurial information professionals and organizations. Its aim is to encourage information professionals at all levels in the organization to understand and engage creatively with innovation, and to realize the benefits of entrepreneurial action. The book invites all information professionals to develop their capacity to act entrepreneurially and to fully explore the full potential of innovation both for their own careers and in the interests of the success of their organizations. Its underlying philosophy is built on an acknowledgement of the considerable change and innovation that has been achieved in information organizations through the opening decades of the digital age, tempered by a belief that a future in which all information resources – including books and archives – will be accessed in digital format, poses even greater challenges for information professionals and organizations. The ability to move into uncharted territory, engage in and enjoy innovation, create radical new visions and manage resources in risky environments will be an essential prerequisite for the survival of organizations and for the career advancement of individuals.

Since in many contexts information organizations are in the public sector and information professionals have a responsibility to contribute to the sustainability and cultural, social, educational and economic development of their communities, information innovators are social innovators and social entrepreneurs. Social or public entrepreneurs seek to generate 'social value' for the communities that they serve, in contrast to traditional business entrepreneurs whose primary aim is profit. Social innovations are essentially concerned with 'making the world a better place', through, for example, improving access to basic resources, supporting disadvantaged groups, and improving quality of life. Despite its different focus, social or public entrepreneurship requires no less ambition, dedication and drive on the part of the individual. Indeed, social innovators often work in contexts where they have limited access to resources, and they therefore need to exert high levels of persuasion, leadership and inspiration in accessing and optimizing the impact of human, financial and political resources.

Innovation is widely discussed in the context of business and economic development. Innovation is associated with organizational survival and growth and, arguably more importantly, a lack of innovation leads to stagnation and decline. In the information industry where there have been major changes resulting from the digitization of information resources, information-rich process, access to information resources, and the way in which those resources are created, shared, distributed, used and exploited, the innovation imperative is emblazoned in neon lights. This means that all information organizations need to embrace, each in their own unique way, innovation, creativity and entrepreneurial spirit and action. Within these organizations, some people will be better at some aspects of the innovation process than others. Some may be good at seeing opportunities and developing ideas, others may be better at sifting and selecting the best idea to develop further and yet others may have a flair for design, or for organizing implementation. Different people have different contributions to make, and those contributions may vary with the nature and type of innovation. So, there is no easy answer to the obvious (and necessary) questions:

1 What innovations should my information organization be engaging in now and planning for the future?
2 What is the optimal process for managing those innovations?

Nevertheless, these are good questions (none of the best questions have easy answers!). The purpose of this book is to assist you in finding your own answers for the context in which you find yourself. Its objective is to offer a set of ideas, examples, concepts and frameworks, and thereby to place both action and sharing of best practice in respect of innovation, entrepreneurship and creativity firmly on the agenda.

The book is designed as a companion volume to the widely acclaimed *Managing Information Services* (Roberts and Rowley, 2004), and *Leadership: the challenge for the information profession* (Roberts and Rowley, 2008). As such it shares the philosophical foundations and specific features of these companion works and is grounded on an underpinning philosophy that theory and practice should be tightly intertwined. Theoretical models and concepts have their foundations in practice. The applications of theories and concepts can assist in sense making, communication, sharing and analysis. They can act as frameworks for the articulation and sharing of best practice, and can promote shared learning. Such application of theory in its turn advances and develops theory to allow it to accommodate a wider variety of contexts, and to evolve in line with practice. The style throughout is one of enquiry rather than instruction.

The first chapter introduces the concepts of 'innovation', 'entrepreneurship' and 'creativity', and argues the case for further reflection on innovation processes and a high level of innovation orientation in information organizations. Chapters 2 and 3 summarize a range of theoretical concepts from the literatures of innovation and entrepreneurship respectively. Chapter 2 examines the nature of innovation and helps the reader to recognize and categorize their innovative actions and decisions, and understand innovation orientation, management, diffusion and adoption. Chapter 3 turns to the concept of entrepreneurship, starting with an exploration of the types of entrepreneurship, including, importantly, public sector corporate entrepreneurship and social entrepreneurship. Subsequent sections explore views of the characteristics and competencies of entrepreneurs, and a variety of aspects of becoming and succeeding as an entrepreneur.

The final two chapters focus on innovation and entrepreneurship within organizational contexts. Chapter 4 explores a number of aspects of how organizations can facilitate entrepreneurship and innovation, including the concept of innovation orientation, the characteristics of an innovative organization, innovative climate and culture, and creativity in organizations. It also discusses leadership for innovation, a variety of aspects of building innovative and creative teams, innovation and entrepreneurship strategies, and readiness and change management. Finally, Chapter 5 discusses innovation in practice in greater detail, starting by outlining the stages in the innovation project. It continues with consideration of the opportunities offered by, and the processes associated with, customer and user involvement in innovation, and collaborative and open innovation through networks and partnerships, respectively. The chapter concludes with some thoughts on the wider challenge for information organizations, contributing to innovation in the public sector and beyond.

The book features:

1 *Learning objectives*: Study objectives are identified at the beginning of each chapter.

2 *Summary and conclusions*: These review the content of each chapter and draw together the key themes that have been developed in each chapter.

3 *Reflections*: Reflection points are distributed throughout each chapter. These are intended to encourage the reader to pause and think about the text. They can also be used as group discussion points.

4 *Review questions*: Review questions appear at the end of each chapter. These are examination-type assessment questions designed to encourage readers to review, interpret and apply the material in the chapter. They provide an opportunity to test retention. The questions also flag the key issues that are addressed in each chapter, and in that sense provide an additional summary of key themes. Although all questions can be answered from the material in this book, better answers will also draw illustration from professional practice and experience, and concepts from wider reading.

5 *Challenges*: Each chapter has a list of challenge questions. These should not be confused with the review questions. Although the basic concepts for thinking about the questions are embedded in the text of the respective chapter, these Challenge questions are designed to provoke further investigation, discussion and debate. There are no easy answers to these questions; they are precisely the imponderable questions that information innovators and researchers know to be at the heart of practice and theory, but for which if there is an answer it will be contingent on the context, and likely to change tomorrow.

6 *Group discussion topics*: These topics are designed to

encourage group discussion and application of the ideas in each chapter in relation to specific organizational practices and contexts. They are specifically designed to invite reflection from staff at all levels in the information organization, with a view to engaging all staff in the innovation process. Such reflection and discussion of innovation processes will enhance the learning from innovation, and thereby develop the organization's innovation competencies and capacity.

7 *References and additional reading*: Sources cited in the text and other useful sources, including as appropriate both print documents and websites, are listed at the end of each chapter.

Audience

The book is designed for information innovators and aspiring information innovators who wish to promote their practice and contribute to the creation of information organizations that succeed through innovation and entrepreneurial action.

References

Mason, F. M. (1989) Libraries, Entrepreneurship, and Risk, *Journal of Library Administration*, **10** (2/3), 169–83.

Riggs, D. E. (2001) The Crisis and Opportunities in Library Leadership, *Journal of Library Administration*, **32** (3/4), 5–17.

Roberts, S. and Rowley, J. (2004) *Managing Information Services*, Facet Publishing.

Roberts, S. and Rowley, J. (2008) *Leadership: the challenge for the information profession*, Facet Publishing.

1

Innovation and entrepreneurship in information organizations

Learning objectives

After reading this chapter you should be able to:

- Explain why innovation is important for information organizations, and understand the range of different types of, and approaches to, innovation.
- Understand the potential relevance of entrepreneurship and entrepreneurial action to information organizations.
- Reflect on the notion of creativity and consider its place in information organizations.
- Discuss the difference between a perspective based on change management and one based on entrepreneurship, innovation and creativity.
- Reflect on the challenges and opportunities for promoting innovation in information organizations.

1.1 Introduction

Information organizations of all kinds (such as libraries, publishers, subscription agents, and information and advice services) have changed significantly in recent years. Achieving these changes has involved high levels of innovation. Some of these innovations are driven directly by the opportunities provided by new technology innovations from other organizations, coupled with changes in consumer expectations and behaviours (e.g. access to full text of journals through Google as a search engine). Others are facilitated by information technology, but driven by policy and marketplace change (e.g. self-issue of books, institutional repositories). Other innovations are not particularly affected by technology platforms, but represent, for example, innovations in community involvement, such as new services for disadvantaged groups and the organization of bibliotherapy reading groups.

Despite there being a hive of activity, and regular reporting on achievements in the popular and professional press (the outcomes of innovation processes), there has been little discussion of innovation and its processes in the information management professional or academic literature. This means that there is limited opportunity to learn from one another's successes and mistakes, and that there is little evidence that information innovators are reflecting sufficiently on their innovation processes, and striving to enhance their own capacity and that of their organizations to innovate. Some commentators suggest that this means that (academic) libraries, for example, are too often making changes for change's sake, without proper evaluation of the impact and value of the change, and specifically without sufficient consideration as to how an innovation (even a small innovation) will help the library to fulfil its mission of supporting learning and research across the university community. Even more importantly, information organizations without an innovation lens on their strategies and projects risk overlooking the wider organizational perspective. An innovation strategy would, for example, contribute to the selection, co-ordination and planning of innovations at all levels in the organization. It would also promote a focus on building an innovative, creative and entrepreneurial organizational culture, to facilitate all stages of the innovation process.

Looking to the future, Maness (2006) is not alone when he suggests that Web 2.0 will have substantial implications for libraries and other players in the information industry, such that a paradigm change is on the horizon. Library 2.0 is a user-centred virtual community. While information professionals might act as facilitators and provide support, they are not necessarily responsible for the creation or provision of the content. Users interact with and create resources with one another and with librarians. If, how and when users adopt Web 2.0 technologies could have an important impact on the rationale for and role of libraries and a whole range of other organizations in the information industry. And, if Web 2.0 does not provoke the paradigm change that some predict, then there are a host of other technology-based innovations that have the potential to have a significant impact on libraries, including the e-book and the development of other digital documents and learning resources, open-source initiatives (including open-source software [OSS], open access publishing and open universities) and mobile learning technologies. More parochially, *Resource Description and Access* (RDA) cataloguing rules and cloud-based library management systems will create opportunities to share metadata, processes and practice in new ways. Finally, and arguably most pressing at the time of writing, many countries are facing significant public sector funding cuts over the next few years, and all public sector employees are likely to be under the directive to 'do more for less'. Major shifts in the role of libraries, or, equally importantly, the public perception of the rationale for libraries, will require some sure and swift footed large scale innovation. Not enough information professionals and leaders have experience with such large scale innovations and their associated change processes. Information professionals would be well advised to take any opportunity available to develop their understanding of innovation and their skills in managing innovation processes.

1.2 Innovation
1.2.1 The innovation imperative

Information organizations exist in an environment in which the importance of innovation is widely recognized by organizations, government bodies and other policy-makers. Organizations need to innovate in order to grow, compete, succeed and survive. Innovation is becoming vital to the survival and growth of most organizations. Damanpour summarizes the situation thus:

> Organisations innovate because of pressure from the external
> environment, such as competition, deregulation, isomorphism,
> resource scarcity, and customer demand, or because of an internal
> organisational choice, such as gaining distinctive competencies,
> reaching a higher level of aspiration, and increasing the extent and
> quality of services. Either way the adoption of innovation is intended
> to ensure adaptive behaviour, changing the organisation to maintain
> or improve its performance.
>
> (Damanpour, 2009, 652–3)

The significance of innovation to societies and economies is
evidenced by the range of government initiatives designed to
promote innovations. For example, in the UK, the aptly named
Department for Innovation, Universities and Skills (DIUS) aims to
direct the UK towards a knowledge economy through creativity and
innovation. In Australia, the Department of Innovation, Industry,
Science and Research (DIISR) not only provides support and
advice for Australian ministers and government and administers
legislation, but it also manages various programmes, undertakes
analyses and provides services and advice to the business, science
and research communities. And, the European Parliament has
initiated the European Year of Creativity and Innovation 2009
aiming to achieve the following:

> Raise awareness of the importance of creativity and innovation for
> personal, social and economic development; to disseminate good
> practices; to stimulate education and research, and to promote policy
> debate on related issues.
>
> (Europa, 2009)

However, despite this growing acknowledgement of the importance
of innovation, there is evidence that many organizations have a
distance to travel in understanding and managing innovation and

innovation processes. For example, a relatively recent study by Cottam, Ensor and Band (2001) suggests that although most UK companies are aware of the importance of innovation to their competitive position, they are not committed to it and further do not know how to commit to an innovative approach. This implies that organizations have a long way to go to optimize their innovation performance and the contribution that innovation can make to their organizational performance. Information organizations, then, are not alone in their need to examine and focus on the development of their innovation management practices.

The following subsections explore the nature of innovation and its link to opportunity seeking, offer some examples of innovation in information organizations and provide some preliminary comments on the management of innovation. Chapter 2 develops the theme of innovation further, with more discussion of different types of innovation, and the innovation process and its management.

1.2.2 Defining innovation

Arguably, one of the difficulties in understanding and managing innovation is the diverse and contextual nature of innovation. Innovations can be small scale and local, or they may involve whole organizations in complete shifts in their strategic direction. This can lead to some confusion as to the exact nature of innovation. Accordingly, the concept of innovation has a number of different definitions. Yet, it is important when considering innovation in an information organization to develop some shared view of what constitutes an innovation. We draw a few definitions of innovation together here in order to explore the question: 'What is innovation?' The definitions that follow present some differing perspectives on the nature of innovation. We conclude with the definition of innovation that we shall be adopting in this book.

A good starting point is Thompson's (1965, 2) early and

straightforward definition, which simply states that 'Innovation is the generation, acceptance and implementation of new ideas, processes, products or services.' A similar definition of innovation was proposed more recently by West and Anderson (1996) and quoted by Wong, Tjosvold and Liu (2009, 239): 'Innovation can be defined as the effective application of processes and products new to the organization and designed to benefit it and its stakeholders.' This definition introduces the notion of benefits to the organization and its stakeholders. Other definitions, such as that offered by Jayanthi and Kingshuk (1998, 472), focus on the idea of newness, and specifically the subjectivity of 'newness', and the need to understand newness in context: 'As long as the idea is perceived as new to the people involved, it is an "innovation" even though it may appear to others to be an "imitation" of something that exists elsewhere.' Some definitions, such as that proposed by Tang (1998, 298), see innovation in terms of projects towards specific innovations: 'Innovation is a process of raising and doing projects with the aim of commercializing or utilizing an innovative product, process or service.'

On the other hand, Damanpour's much quoted definition of innovation focuses on innovation as a means of changing an organization, and emphasizes the role of its external environment in provoking and shaping those changes:

> Innovation is conceived as a means of changing an organization, either as a response to changes in the external environment or as a pre-emptive action to influence the environment. Hence, innovation is here broadly defined to encompass a range of types, including new product or service, new process technology, new organization structure or administrative systems, or new plans or programmes pertaining to organization members.
>
> (Damanpour, 1996, 694)

Other variations in the definition of innovation arise from different disciplinary perspectives. For example, in knowledge management, the focus is on knowledge being vital for innovation:

> Innovation is the creation of new knowledge and ideas to facilitate new business outcomes, aimed at improving internal business processes and structures and to create market driven products and services. Innovation encompasses both radical and incremental innovation.
>
> (Plessis, 2007, 21)

Finally, we introduce the definition of innovation that will be used throughout this book. This definition was created from an analysis of many earlier definitions of innovation, and is intended to provide an interdisciplinary and all-encompassing definition of innovation:

> Innovation is the multi-stage process whereby organizations transform ideas into new/improved products, services or processes, in order to advance, compete and differentiate themselves successfully in their marketplace.
>
> (Baregheh, Rowley and Sambrook, 2009, 1334)

Reflect: *One way of measuring how innovative an organization is, is to count the number of innovations that it has completed in, say, the last year. Make a list of the innovations that your organization has implemented in the last year (reviewing a newsletter or annual report might help). What are the problems with this innovation counting approach to the measurement of innovation performance? Can you suggest any alternative approaches to measurement?*

1.2.3 Innovation in practice

Innovation takes a number of different guises and scales. Table 1.1 offers an assorted collection of recent innovations in information organizations. Some innovations, such as the introduction of self-issue systems, or the introduction of radio-frequency identification

Table 1.1 *Examples of recent innovations in information organizations*

Organization	Innovation
Open University Library Service	Placing the library at the hub of the Open University's distance learning services – taking the service to where the user is.
National Health Service (NHS) Quality Improvement Scotland	The use of Web 2.0 technologies for current awareness in healthcare.
Leeds Library and Information Service	Across the Board: autism support for families.
School libraries	Providing access to digital resources to support learning in art, English, history, modern languages and science.
Winchester Discovery Centre	New and innovative public library building/community space.
University of Hertfordshire	Rebranding and positioning of information staff as Knowledge and Business Intelligence Consultants.
Academic libraries	Introduction of self-issue systems.
Public libraries	Development of therapeutic reading groups.
Esher College	Use and development of Microsoft Office SharePoint technology as part of a managed learning environment.
Hillingdon Public Libraries	Partnerships with high profile brands, such as Starbucks and Apple iMacs.
Academic libraries, publishers, universities and others	Changes in scholarly publishing models, including open-access initiatives.
British Broadcasting Corporation (BBC)	Making previously internal digital resources available free to the public.

(RFID), are driven by opportunities offered by the development of technologies. Others, such as the growing importance of evidence-based practice in health libraries, are driven by changes in government or public sector policies. In such instances, it is likely that many libraries in a specific sector will be attempting similar innovations more or less simultaneously. In other instances, such as the design and construction of a new building, the timing of the innovation may vary significantly between libraries, depending upon local opportunities and needs. Many innovations within libraries are part of a wider pattern of innovation across the information and digital industries. For example, in initiatives to encourage reading, public and school libraries will be working with a range of other agencies and groups, and, in their endeavours to move to a world of digital information resources, academic libraries are part of a wider landscape that includes publishers, search engine providers, subscriptions agents, authors, editors and national libraries. Such a complex network of innovations of different types and extents provides plenty of opportunity for benchmarking and learning from others. It is important that such benchmarking does not only address the details of the innovation (e.g. how to design a current awareness service for a consultancy firm), but also the innovation process.

Innovation is a process, and a process that does not just happen, but which needs managing. The innovation process involves a number of stages, and all innovation requires:

- ideas and opportunities
- selection of 'good' ideas for further development
- development of selected ideas into new products, services, processes, or ways of working or other innovations
- co-ordination across functions
- management of knowledge, financial, human and operational resources
- communication and engagement with customers.

One of the big challenges of innovation is integration and co-ordination across functions. Typically organizations are structured to facilitate their existing tasks; this means that they may not be well structured to facilitate, for example, communication, team-working and resource allocation for innovation. Further, there is a tension associated with continuing to do what the organization has always done, alongside innovation.

There is evidence that some organizations are better at successful innovation than others; such organizations may be described as inno-vation oriented. In such innovation-oriented organizations, innovation – and associated processes, such as learning – are embedded in the culture and strategy of the organization; innovation and entrepreneurship are encouraged and welcomed, but they are also managed so as to generate outcomes that contribute towards the organization's ongoing success.

Innovation in practice, then, involves both specific project management to select, design and implement a specific innovation, and also the promotion of an organizational culture that encourages and facilitates innovation. These themes are developed further in Chapters 2, 4 and 5.

1.3 Entrepreneurship
1.3.1 Linking innovation and entrepreneurship

Successful innovation requires individuals with the ability to see and take advantage of opportunities, being prepared to challenge and change, possessing a willingness to take risks, an ability to enthuse and engage others and a focused and determined drive to succeed. In other words, innovation requires entrepreneurial attitudes and activities, or entrepreneurship.

Innovation and entrepreneurship are, then, tightly coupled; it is not possible to discuss one without the other. There are two separate literatures, but these are complementary. The innovation literature tends to focus on the processes associated with the development of new products, services and processes, and has a strong interface with the literature on research and development processes; the underlying context for much of the discussion and operationalization of innovation is large organizations. Entrepreneurship, on the other hand, is more traditionally associated with start-up businesses that are typically small. The word 'entrepreneur' comes from the 17th-century French word *entreprendre*, which refers to people who 'undertook' the risk of new enterprise. As we shall discuss further in Chapter 3, early theories of entrepreneurship, such as those developed by Schumpeter, focused on the role of the entrepreneur as an agent for change in economic systems. However, more recently, commentators have taken increasing interest in the entrepreneurial process, and, most interestingly for our purpose, entrepreneurial behaviour. The impact of such behaviour is not restricted solely to economic outcomes, but may also lead to social, technological and cultural outcomes. Both innovation and entrepreneurship are important in all types of organizations and communities.

This section on entrepreneurship explains the link between entrepreneurship and innovation. It discusses different types of entrepreneurship and identifies social and public entrepreneurship as being of most interest to information organizations. Chapter 3 develops the theme of entrepreneurship further, with a more detailed discussion of the different types of entrepreneurship and a particular focus on entrepreneurial characteristics and behaviours.

1.3.2 Defining entrepreneurship

Before proceeding, it is useful to reflect on what is meant by the terms 'entrepreneurship' and 'entrepreneur'. As with innovation, there are many varying definitions of entrepreneurship and as many different approaches to describing the traits, behaviour and competences of entrepreneurs, so the answer to the question: 'What is entrepreneurship?' is not straightforward. Here are four definitions that are good, because they focus on entrepreneurship as being associated with taking opportunities, and emphasize the link between entrepreneurship and innovation:

* 'The discovery, evaluation, and utilization of future goods and services' (Murphy, Liao and Welsch, 2006, 29).
* 'Turning ideas into a success, being imaginative, creative, inventive, problem solving and can even just be about making things more interesting' (see www.nwda.co.uk).
* 'Entrepreneurship is a way of thinking, reasoning, and acting that is opportunity driven' (Morrisette and Schraeder, 2007, 15).
* 'Entrepreneurship is the process by which individuals pursue opportunities without regard to resources they currently

control. The essence of entrepreneurial behaviour is identifying opportunities and putting useful ideas into practice' (Barringer and Ireland, 2008, 6).

Recently, there has been an increasing focus on what Rae (2007) refers to as 'opportunity-centred entrepreneurship'. Rae suggests that opportunity-centred entrepreneurship involves four interconnected themes: personal enterprise (relating an opportunity to personal goals); creating and exploring the opportunity; planning to realize it; and acting to make it happen. Complementary to this is Sorensen, Lassen and Hinson's (2007) suggestion that entrepreneurship is a 'social journey of opportunity construction'. They suggest that the entrepreneurial process is an interaction between:

- *voluntarist* (willing) individuals
- their *social networks* – emphasizing that no individual can construct, evaluate or exploit entrepreneurial opportunities without others (such as customers, bankers, suppliers and/or colleagues)
- *structures* associated with objectifying the opportunity, or translating it into a form that others can understand and engage with
- *the physical context* of the entrepreneurial process, which generates a variety of barriers and facilitators as the process unfolds.

Comments from other important writers focus on the entrepreneur, the person who delivers on entrepreneurship. These commentators also emphasize the link between entrepreneurship and innovation. Drucker's (1998) perspective is that successful entrepreneurs have a commitment to the systematic practice of innovation, or to the effort to create purposeful, focused change in an enterprise's economic or social potential. Rae (2007) describes an entrepreneur as a person who acts in an enterprising way (using skills, knowledge and personal attributes to apply creative ideas and innovations to practical situations) and who creates and acts on an opportunity. Bessant and Tidd (2007) suggest the concept of the innovative entrepreneur. Such individuals are driven by the desire to create or change something, whether in the private, public or third sectors. Independence, wealth and reputation (all possible outcomes of entrepreneurship) are not these people's primary goals; their main motivation is to change something or to actually create something new. Two important categories of innovative entrepreneurs are social entrepreneurs and technological entrepreneurs. Both of these categories are pertinent to information organizations, and are discussed next.

Reflect: Have you ever 'spotted an opportunity'? What did you do about it? Make a short list of the negative and positive consequences of your action.

1.3.3 Entrepreneurship in information organizations

On account of its association with starting a new business, and other commercial activities, entrepreneurship has too often been viewed as of limited interest to public and academic libraries. Indeed, there is limited mention of entrepreneurship in the information literature. The most common mention of entrepreneurship in relation to libraries arises in association with the surges of interest in fund-raising activities in libraries, which are acknowledged to require enterprise (e.g. Nicholson, 1992; and, Riggs, 1989). More recently, there have been occasional contributions that discuss the role of libraries in contributing to local and regional economic, community and cultural development (Li, 2006) and as cultural entrepreneurs delivering four types of experiences: entertainment, education, escapist and aesthetic (Nijboer, 2006). Overall, however, there has been insufficient attention focused on the creation of entrepreneurial cultures at organizational level and entrepreneurial behaviours and competencies at individual level.

The broadening of the concept of entrepreneurship to embrace entrepreneurship in a variety of different contexts is of particular relevance to public sector information organizations. This has led to the proposal of concepts such as 'corporate entrepreneurship' and 'intrapreneurship', 'social entrepreneurship', 'public entrepreneurship', 'digital entrepreneurship', 'technology entrepreneurship' and 'knowledge entrepreneurship', all of which have a role in information organizations. Here we explain each of these terms briefly, and return to discuss them in more detail in Chapter 3:

Corporate entrepreneurship and intrapreneurship

Corporate entrepreneurship is concerned with acting entrepreneurially in an existing, often large, organization, and is often associated with change and innovation:

> Corporate entrepreneurship can be defined as the effort of promoting innovation from an internal organizational perspective, through the assessment of potential new opportunities, alignment of resources, exploitation and commercialisation of said opportunities.
>
> (McFadzean, O'Loughlin and Shaw, 2005, 352)

Corporate entrepreneurship is sometimes regarded as synonymous with *intrapreneurship*, since both are concerned with entrepreneurship within an existing organization. However, Antoncic and Hisrich (2003) make a differentiation between the two terms on the basis that corporate entrepreneurship implies that the organization is typically a large commercial organization, whereas intrapreneurship can apply to any organization, and its scope, while including other innovative activities and orientations, may also embrace the formation of new ventures. They suggest that intrapreneurship may include: 'new business venturing, product/service innovation, process innovation, self-renewal, risk taking, proactiveness, and competitive aggressiveness' (Antoncic and Hisrich, 2003, 9).

Public and social entrepreneurship

Public entrepreneurship is an attempt to broaden the notion of entrepreneurship from its focus on profit making, to embrace its role in innovation towards the availability and delivery of public services that augment social capital (Zampetakis and Moustakis, 2007). Caruana, Ewing and Ramaseshan (2002), for example, suggest that 'public sector entities can provide new value to the various stakeholders they serve by adopting an entrepreneurial approach with the resources over which they have control'. And Morris and Jones (1999, 74) suggest that public sector entrepreneurship is: 'the process of creating value for citizens by bringing together unique combinations of public and/or private resources to exploit social opportunities'.

Social entrepreneurship is distinguished from commercial entrepreneurship by its focus on the creation of 'social value' rather than on the generation of profit or wealth. According to the Ashoka Foundation (www.ashoka.org) (the non-profit organization for encouraging social entrepreneurship) social entrepreneurs are: 'individuals with innovative solutions to society's most pressing social problems. They are ambitious and persistent, tackling major social issues and offering new ideas for wide-scale change.'

It is important to appreciate that social entrepreneurship is more than just philanthropy or good works, and is targeted at creating long-term sustainable change rather than a short-term alleviation of problems. The most notable examples of social entrepreneurship involve new non-profit venture creation by individuals with drive and vision, but social entrepreneurship can be conducted within existing non-profit, public sector and business organizations. Increasingly, both social enterprises and businesses are concerned with 'more-than-profit', and use blended business value models that combine revenue and profit generation with the generation of social value. During the 19th and 20th centuries some of the most successful entrepreneurs have straddled the public and private sectors and led to innovations in mainstream public services such as education, the arts and healthcare.

Social entrepreneurship and public entrepreneurship are linked, since social value, it might be argued, should be the outcome of public entrepreneurship. But social entrepreneurship is not restricted to public sector organizations and, equally importantly, public sector organizations have specific mandates, processes, structures and systems which may constrain their scope for the creation of social value.

Digital, knowledge and technology entrepreneurship

Digital entrepreneurship is associated with the leverage of new technologies in ways that create new commercial opportunities, disseminate information and support collaboration, communication and community building.

Knowledge entrepreneurship is associated with seeking opportunities and taking action in order to realize an innovative knowledge practice or product. Knowledge entrepreneurship might either lead to a knowledge-based product or service for the marketplace, or it might focus on the promotion of organizational learning to support organizational change and innovation (Rowley, 2000). For example, in taking the second of these two perspectives Skrzeszewski (2006, 3) defines a knowledge entrepreneur thus: 'someone who is skilled at creating and using intellectual assets for the development of new ventures or services that will lead to personal and community wealth creation or to improved and enhanced services'.

Technological entrepreneur is a term most usually applied to refer to those responsible for small start-up technology companies, which may grow into much larger businesses. Such entrepreneurs are an important part of the information industry, and include such names as Bill Gates (Microsoft), Larry Page and Sergey Brinn (YouTube), and Steve and Julie Pankhurst (Friends Reunited).

Reflect: Identify a list of people who you would describe as entrepreneurs. Which of the labels above would most apply to each of the people in your list?

Reflect: Look at the characteristics of entrepreneurs listed in Figure 1.1. Are you (or have you been, or might you become) an entrepreneur?

Bessant and Tidd (2007) suggest that some of the key characteristics of an entrepreneur are:

1 a passion for seeking new opportunities and ways to profit from change or disruption
2 a pursuit of opportunities with focus on a limited number of projects, rather than being distracted by every option
3 a focus on action and execution, avoiding endless analysis
4 involving and energizing networks of relationships, exploiting the expertise and resources of others, while helping others to achieve their own goals.

Figure 1.1 *Are you an entrepreneur?*

1.4 Creativity

Central to both innovation and entrepreneurship is the process of generating and developing ideas, or creativity. Creativity lies at the heart of the idea development process. Bessant and Tidd define creativity as:

> Creativity is the making and communicating of meaningful new connections to help us think of many possibilities, to help us think and experience in varied ways and using different points of view; to help us think of new and unusual possibilities and to guide us in generating and selecting alternatives. These new connections and possibilities must result in something of value for the individual, group, organization, or society.
>
> (Bessant and Tidd, 2007, 40)

In traditional models of the stages of innovation, creative idea generation is often seen as the first stage in the innovation process, and is associated with the generation of new ideas: 'Creativity is the process of generating a novel or useful idea' (Barringer and Ireland, 2008, 45).

From this perspective, discussions of creativity in entrepreneurship and innovation tend to focus on idea generation. From the perspective of the individual, Barringer and Ireland (2008) discuss creativity in terms of the following stages:

1 *Preparation*: the background, experience and knowledge that the individual brings to the opportunity recognition process.
2 *Incubation*: during which a person thinks about a problem, or 'mulls over' it, either consciously or unconsciously.
3 *Insight*: the flash of recognition when the solution to a problem is seen or an idea is born.
4 *Evaluation*: when an idea is subjected to scrutiny and analysed for its viability and potential.
5 *Elaboration*: when the idea is put into a final form, the details are worked out and the idea is transformed into a new product, service or business concept.

Such models are interesting as they elaborate a structure that can assist in thinking about the creative thinking process. However, they tend to be 'front-end creative'. It is preferable to subscribe to the view that creativity is essential throughout the idea development process, as proposed by Bragg and Bragg (2005). Bragg and Bragg suggest a four-stage idea development process, which includes seeking and shaping opportunities, generating new ideas, evaluating and selecting ideas, and planning for implementation, and argue that creativity is essential throughout the innovation and entrepreneurial process. Further, successful ideas do not just emerge, they need cultivating and developing. The 'type' of creativity required at different stages in the process may differ, and typically involves a combination of intuition and imagination (divergent thinking) and logic and systems (convergent thinking); it may therefore need to draw on the differing creative talents of a range of people. Table 1.2 shows the relative importance of

Table 1.2 *Creative thinking styles through the idea development process (Bragg and Bragg, 2005, 43)*

Step	Description	Thinking style
1 Seeking and shaping opportunities.	Identifying and exploring different opportunities, followed by analytical judgement.	Divergent and convergent thinking equally dominant.
2 Generating new ideas.	Creating significant volumes of innovative, imaginative and associative ideas.	Divergent thinking is dominant.
3 Evaluating and selecting ideas.	Screening the best from the rest and then evaluating those few in detail.	Convergent thinking is dominant.
4 Planning for implementation.	Identifying and overcoming blocks to implementation.	Divergent and convergent thinking equally dominant.

divergent and convergent thinking at the different stages in the idea development process.

Creativity is not restricted to people who have 'creative' jobs, such as those that include design, development and advertising, but is an orientation towards the novel, and is based on a belief in the ability to produce creative outcomes. Personality traits often associated with creativity include: openness to experience, tolerance of ambiguity, resistance to premature closure, curiosity and risk taking. They also include creative thinking abilities, such as fluency, flexibility, originality and elaboration (Bessant and Tidd, 2007).

While we all have the potential to be creative, we engage with that potential to varying extents and express our creativity in different ways. Although some individuals may be viewed as being more creative than others, it is possible for most people to improve their creative productivity. Organizations have an important role in promoting individual creativity through conscious attention to the organizational climate and its impact on creativity, the environment in which people work, the projects, opportunities and challenges that people experience and the structures, systems, policies and techniques that support and influence their working practices. An individual or team's level of creativity may depend crucially on context. So, it may not be possible to identify a person as more or less creative. Rather, as Bessant and Tidd suggest (2007, 43), the question should be: 'Creative at what, when, how, where, why, and with whom?'

Reflect: Make a list of some changes in your working context that you feel might increase your creative productivity.

1.5 What's new about innovation?

As discussed in Section 1.1, information organizations have changed significantly in recent years, in response to the challenges and opportunities resulting largely from the digitization of information resources. To achieve these changes organizations and individuals will have been engaged in many change processes, and will have developed a level of expertise in engaging in, managing and leading change. So, what is the difference between change management and innovation? And what is the relevance of the body of expertise that has been gained through these experiences to innovation? This section seeks to provide some answers to these questions.

An innovation is a change, in a product, service, process or, more widely, an organization. Innovation management therefore shares much in common with change management. It might be argued at one level that successful innovation is dependent on successful change management. And in both change management and innovation it is important to work with the people who will be affected by or involved in the change or innovation, and to provide leadership, confidence and inspiration. Indeed, as part of the discussion of organizing for innovation in Chapter 4, a subsection on launching into an internal market, or change management, is included. So, the shift from a focus on change to a focus on innovation can be viewed as a matter of emphasis and perspective.

On this basis, change can be differentiated from innovation thus:

- Literature on change management tends to assume that change leaders and change agents either know what change is necessary, or are able, through collaboration and consultation, to arrive at a compromise that specifies what needs to happen. Innovation has greater potential to be both bottom-up and top-down.
- Innovation applies to changes to products, services, processes and organizations; change management tends towards a more internal focus, often with an emphasis on people (employees) and processes.
- Partly on account of its emphasis on 'newness' and 'novelty', taking an innovation perspective as opposed to a change perspective tends to strengthen the emphasis on the ideas generation phase of a development.
- The innovation literature directs greater attention to the organizational environment than does the change literature. Innovation starts with ideas. Those ideas are filtered and selected on the basis of their capacity to enhance organizational performance, whether that be measured in terms of revenue and profit or in terms of social value and impact on and contribution to communities.

Reflect: Is innovation a facet of change, or is change a facet of innovation?

1.6 Promoting innovation in information organizations

One of the very real challenges to many information organizations is that innovators and entrepreneurs do not perform well in bureaucracies, and public sector organizations are often mired in bureaucracies with over-prescriptive accounting systems, overburdened IT departments and lack of discretionary time and money (Best, 2001). There may be a need for innovations and entrepreneurial action throughout the organization, and arguably radical, paradigm innovation, but potential innovators need a well honed pair of scissors and a lot of patience to find their way through the 'red tape'. Many public sector organizations have neither the culture nor the structure to effectively support change, creativity, innovation and entrepreneurship. They are risk averse, quoting public accountability as a defence, and often find it difficult to release resources to support imaginative and substantial innovation. Some argue that the culture of control that is ingrained in such organizations is at odds with innovation. One blogger observed that Google give staff 20% of their working time to engage in developing their own ideas. How many library managers would dare to implement such a scheme? (And would they lose their job if they did?)

Nevertheless, there is hope, and evidence that entrepreneurial behaviour can surface. For example, in the UK there is evidence that public service is changing rapidly, with a reinforced focus on citizen and community, underpinned by a network in public services (Communities and Local Government, 2008; Taylor and Pask, 2008). Information professionals need to play an active role in such developments, to grasp the opportunity to embrace innovation and entrepreneurial action, and develop, deliver and promote their role as public sector entrepreneurs. The Elsevier Foundation, under its Innovative Libraries in Developing Countries Program, awards grants to innovative libraries in developing countries (Africa, Asia and Latin America) to enhance library infrastructure, expand library information resources, offer training and education programmes and support partnerships (http://elsevierfoundation.org). Griffin (2008) describes initiatives under this programme that variously improve how information is used to combat AIDS, assist with agriculture development and support patient healthcare. In the US, the Special Libraries Association is establishing Library Innovation Labs, focusing on promoting technology innovation. In one of the few published studies on public entrepreneurship, Zampetakis and Moustakis (2007) found facets of entrepreneurial behaviour in frontline staff in the relatively traditional Greek public sector. They noted, in particular, evidence of the impact of a supportive context, such as encouragement of initiatives and access to managerial information on entrepreneurial behaviour among public servants. Key antecedents of entrepreneurial behaviour were identified as 'creation of an energetic working environment', 'change orientation' and 'strategic vision'.

Reflect: What are the most significant constraints upon your acting entrepreneurially? What could you do to lessen the effect of these constraints?

Summary and conclusions

This chapter has introduced the innovation imperative, and has explored the various meanings associated with the concepts of innovation, entrepreneurship and creativity that will re-emerge in various guises throughout this book. It has commented on the tight linkage between these three concepts, and has discussed the relationship between innovation management and change management. More specifically, this chapter has commenced the discussion on the need for innovation in its various guises in organizations, and the value of innovative organizational cultures and a systematic approach to innovation management. Further, it has noted the importance of appreciating that entrepreneurship is not just applicable in business organizations, but also has a role, in the form of public and social entrepreneurship, in creating value for communities. Creativity is central to both innovation and entrepreneurship and should not be viewed as being restricted to specific roles or stages in the innovation process.

The last two sections in this chapter explore some key aspects of innovation management for information organizations. The first of these explores the difference between change management and innovation management, suggesting that information organizations should use their experience with change management as a platform to develop innovation management capacity. The final section acknowledges some of the challenges of the cultivation of innovation and entrepreneurship in information organizations, many of which are public sector organizations, and offers a platform for further discussion of these challenges and their negotiation in later chapters (specifically Chapters 3 and 4).

Review questions

1 What are the potential benefits to information organizations of a more proactive approach to the facilitation and management of innovation?
2 Choose the definition of innovation that makes most sense to you. Explain why you have selected it.
3 How would you describe: (a) entrepreneurship and (b) an entrepreneur?
4 Discuss the different types of entrepreneurship that have been proposed, and explain why each concept is useful.
5 What do you understand by the term 'creativity'? Why is it important to both innovation and entrepreneurship?
6 What is the difference between change management and promoting and managing innovation in information organizations?
7 Discuss some of the initiatives that are underway to promote innovation in libraries and other information organizations.

Challenges

1 How can an information professional identify the most important innovations for the survival and success of their organization?
2 What is and what is not an innovation? How new does something have to be to be regarded as an innovation?
3 To what extent can entrepreneurship be learned?
4 Is it necessary to differentiate between different types of entrepreneurship and entrepreneurs?
5 How can creativity be cultivated and applied in specific contexts?
6 How can public sector organizations adapt their culture, systems and processes to facilitate innovation, entrepreneurship and creativity?

Group discussion topics

Group discussion topic 1: Future innovations

1 Discuss what you think will be the next big innovation that will impact on the information industry.

Group discussion topic 2: Capitalizing on opportunities

1 In relation to a recent innovation that you have been involved with:
- What were the personal circumstances or drivers that led you to seek an opportunity to do things differently?
- How did you go about locating and developing that opportunity/idea?
- How did you go about the planning for translating that opportunity into action?
- How did you go about capitalizing on the new opportunity?

Group discussion topic 3: Entrepreneurship in information organizations

1 What do you see as the primary outcome(s) of entrepreneurship in information organizations? (Or: Why is entrepreneurship beneficial in information organizations?)
2 Do you perceive there to be conflict in seeking to generate revenue and social value simultaneously?
3 Identify two information professionals who you would regard as successful entrepreneurs. What have they achieved and how?

References and additional reading

Antoncic, B. and Hisrich, R. D. (2003) Clarifying the Intrapreneurship Concept, *Journal of Small Business and Enterprise Development*, **10** (1), 7–24.

Baregheh, A., Rowley, J. and Sambrook, S. (2009) Towards a Multidisciplinary Definition of Innovation, *Management Decision*, **47** (8), 1323–39.

Barringer, B. R. and Ireland, R. D. (2008) *Entrepreneurship:*

successfully launching new ventures, 2nd edn, Pearson Prentice Hall.

Bessant, J. and Tidd, J. (2007) *Innovation and Entrepreneurship,* 3rd edn, Wiley.

Best, J. (2001) Supporting the Public Library Entrepreneur, *The Bottom Line: Managing Library Finance,* **14** (3), 132–44.

Bragg, A. and Bragg, M. (2005) *Developing New Business Ideas: a step-by-step guide to creating new business ideas worth backing,* Pearson Education.

Caruana, A., Ewing, M. T. and Ramaseshan, B. (2002) Effects of Some Environmental Challenges and Centralization on the Entrepreneurial Orientation and Performance of Public Sector Entities, *The Service Industries Management Journal,* **22** (2), 43–58.

Communities and Local Government (2008) *Unlocking the Talent of our Communities,* www.communities.gov.uk.

Cottam, A., Ensor, J. and Band, C. (2001) A Benchmark Study of Strategic Commitment to Innovation, *European Journal of Innovation Management,* **4** (2), 88–94.

Damanpour, F. (1996) Organizational Complexity and Innovation: developing and testing multiple contingency models, *Management Science,* **42** (5), 693–716.

Damanpour, F. (2009) Combinative Effects of Innovation Types and Organizational Performance: a longitudinal study of service organizations, *Journal of Management Studies,* **46** (4), 650–75.

Drucker, P. F. (1998) The Discipline of Innovation, *Harvard Business Review,* **76** (6), 149–57.

Drucker, P. (2007) *Innovation and Entrepreneurship,* rev edn, Butterworth Heinemann.

Europa (2009) *About the Year,* http://create2009.europa.eu/about_the_year.html.

Griffin, D. (2008) STM Publisher Gives Grants to Innovative Libraries in the Developing World, *Information World Review,* **18**, February, www.iwr.co.uk.

Jayanthi, S. and Kingshuk, S. K. (1998) Innovation
Implementation in High Technology Manufacturing: a chaos-
theoretic empirical analysis, *Journal of Operations
Management*, **16** (4), 471–94.

Kaplan, J. M. and Warren, A. C. (2007) *Patterns of
Entrepreneurship*, 2nd edn, Wiley.

Knight, G. A. (1997) Firm Orientation and Strategy under
Regional Market Integration, *International Executive*, **39** (3),
351–74.

Leadbetter, C. (1996) *The Rise of the Social Entrepreneur*, Demos.

Li, X. (2006) Library as Incubating Space for Innovations:
practices, trends and skill sets, *Library Management*, **27** (6/7),
370–8.

Lougee, W. P. (2002) *Diffuse Libraries: emergent roles for the
research library in the digital age*,
www.clir.org/pubs/reports/pub108/contents.html.

Mair, J., Robinson, J. and Hockers, K. (2006) *Social
Entrepreneurship*, Palgrave.

Maness, J. M. (2006) Library 2.0 Theory: Web 2.0 and its
implications for libraries, *Webology*, **3** (2),
www.webology.ir/2006/v3n2/a25.html.

Mason, F. M. (1989) Libraries, Entrepreneurship, and Risk,
Journal of Library Administration, **10** (2/3), 169–83.

McFadzean, E., O'Loughlin, A. and Shaw, E. (2005) Corporate
Entrepreneurship and Innovation Part 1: the missing link,
European Journal of Innovation Management, **8** (3), 350–72.

Morris, M. H. and Jones, F. F. (1999) Entrepreneurship in
Established Organisations: the case of the public sector,
Entrepreneurship Theory and Practice, **24** (1), 71–91.

Morrisette, S. and Schraeder, M. (2007) Affirming
Entrepreneurship: the best hope for organizations,
Development and Learning in Organizations, **21** (1), 15–17.

Murphy, P. J., Liao, J. and Welsch, H. P. (2006) A Conceptual
History of Entrepreneurial Thought, *Journal of Management
History*, **12** (1), 12–35.

Nicholson, H. (1992) Uncomfortable Bedfellows: enterprise and academic libraries, *Journal of Librarianship and Information Science*, **24** (1), 9–13.

Nijboer, J. (2006) Cultural Entrepreneurship in Libraries, *New Library World*, **107** (1228/1229), 434–43.

Plessis, M. D. (2007) The Role of Knowledge Management in Innovation, *Journal of Knowledge Management*, **11** (4), 20–9.

Rae, D. (2007) *Entrepreneurship: from opportunity to action*, Palgrave MacMillan.

Riggs, D. E. (1989) *Creativity, Innovation, and Entrepreneurship in Libraries*, Haworth Press.

Riggs, D. E. (2001) The Crisis and Opportunities in Library Leadership, *Journal of Library Administration*, **32** (3/4), 5–17.

Rowley, J. (2000) From Learning Organization to Knowledge Entrepreneur, *Journal of Knowledge Management*, **4** (1), 7–15.

Skrzeszewski, S. (2006) *The Knowledge Entrepreneur*, Scarecrow Press.

Social entrepreneurship, Wikipedia, http://en.wikipedia.org/wiki/Social_entrepreneurship.

Sorensen, S., Lassen, A. H. and Hinson, R. (2007) Towards a Conceptualization of Entrepreneurship, *The Journal of Research in Marketing and Entrepreneurship*, **9**, 89–101.

Tang, H. K. (1998) An Integrative Model of Innovation in Organizations, *Technovation*, **18** (5), 297–309.

Taylor, B. and Pask, R. (2008) *Community Libraries Programme Evaluation*, MLA.

Thompson, V. A. (1965) Bureaucracy and Innovation, *Administrative Science Quarterly*, **10** (1), 1–20.

Tidd, J., Bessant, J. and Pavitt, K. (2005) *Managing Innovation: integrating technological, market and organizational change*, 3rd edn, Wiley.

West, M. A. and Anderson, N. R. (1996) Innovation in Top Management Teams, *Journal of Applied Psychology*, **81** (6), 680–93.

Wickham, P. A. (2006) *Strategic Entrepreneurship*, Prentice Hall.

Wong, A., Tjosvold, D. and Liu, C. (2009) Innovation by Teams in Shanghai: cooperative goals for group confidence and persistence, *British Journal of Management*, **20** (2), 238–51.

Zampetakis, L. A. and Moustakis, V. (2007) Entrepreneurial Behaviour in the Greek Public Sector, *International Journal of Entrepreneurial Behaviour and Research*, **13** (1), 19–38.

2

Innovation
Co-authored by Anahita Baregheh

Learning objectives
After reading this chapter you should be able to:

- Understand the key attributes of 'innovation'.
- Appreciate the need for innovations with different extents and impacts.
- Appreciate the range of different types of innovation, and understand the relationships between them.
- Discuss the role of information systems (IS) in innovation.
- Understand the relevance of 'innovation orientation' for organizations.
- Discuss innovation as a managed process.
- Understand aspects of the innovation diffusion and adoption process.

2.1 Introduction
Chapter 1 offered some preliminary definitions of innovation, and discussed the importance of innovation and change in information organizations. This chapter develops the theme of innovation further by introducing a range of theoretical concepts from the ever expanding literature on innovation. This chapter, together with the chapter that follows on entrepreneurship, is designed to provide a focused overview of concepts and frameworks that can be used by information practitioners to reflect on, articulate and discuss the innovation processes in which they participate, or have responsibility for initiating, planning or promoting.

This chapter commences with a discussion of what can be described as the attributes of innovation; this section introduces a range of innovation concepts that are discussed further later in the chapter. Next, the nature or degree of novelty of innovation is discussed. This is followed by a section that outlines and discusses the different types of innovation, and the relationship between those types of innovation. The subsequent section briefly explores the relationship between information systems and innovation. This is followed by two sections that introduce different aspects of organizing for innovation, innovation orientation and innovation management. The chapter concludes with a discussion of the important concept of innovation diffusion and adoption.

2.2 What is innovation?

In Chapter 1 we discussed how many different definitions of innovation have been put forward, created by different authors at different points in time, and most significantly grounded in different disciplinary perspectives, such as business and management, organization studies, and science and technology. The number and diversity of definitions leads to confusion in relation to the nature of innovation which has consequences both for building knowledge about innovation and for the management of innovation in practice (Ettlie, Bridges and O'Keefe, 1984; McAdam, Reid and Gibson, 2004). Accordingly, in earlier work the author and her colleagues have sought to integrate these definitions and to provide a generic and all-embracing definition. This definition was also introduced in Chapter 1, and is the definition of innovation that we shall use throughout this book:

> Innovation is the multi-stage process whereby organizations transform ideas into new/improved products, services or processes, in order to advance, compete and differentiate themselves successfully in their marketplace.
>
> (Baregheh, Rowley and Sambrook, 2009, 1334)

This definition of innovation is based on an analysis that proposes a number of attributes or aspects of innovation:

- *Aim of innovation*: the overall result that the organization wants to achieve through innovation.
- *Nature of innovation*: the form of the innovation, specifically whether the innovation process results in something new (radical innovation) or improved (incremental innovation).
- *Type of innovation*: the kind of innovation, as in the type of output or the result of innovation, such as a product, service or process.
- *Stages of innovation*: the steps in the innovation process which usually start from idea generation and end with commercialization.
- *Social context*: any social entity, system or group of people involved in the innovation process or other environmental factors affecting the innovation.
- *Means of innovation*: the necessary resources (e.g. technical, creative, financial) that need to be in place in order to progress an innovation.

Together these attributes can be used to define and profile a specific innovation, and to compare it with other innovations. The three most discussed of these attributes – the nature of an innovation, the type of innovation and stages of the innovation – are revisited in more detail in the subsequent sections of this chapter.

Implicit in most definitions of innovation, and also to some extent in the attributes identified above, is the assumption that it is possible to identify a specific innovation. So, for example, if we identify a specific innovation, such as the introduction of an e-books supply service in an academic library, it is then possible to see this as a 'project'. This might allow us to explore the:

- *Aim of the innovation*: to expand access to e-resources for university learners.

- *Nature of the innovation*: radical, in the sense that it involves implementing a new service and introducing a range of new processes.
- *Type of innovation*: service, in the sense that a new service becomes available to users.
- *Stages of the innovation process*: these could be identified, and may, for example, involve generating the idea for the service, designing the service, and implementing the service.
- *Social context of the innovation*: the library and university context within which the innovation is conducted, and specifically the staff and learners who may be affected by the implementation.
- *Means of the innovation*: the resources required and exploited to achieve the development, design and implementation of the new e-book service, including financial, human and IT resources.

This 'project-based' approach to innovation is useful in practice because it makes it easier to focus interest and engagement. But, the identification of individual innovations is not always possible or desirable. First and foremost, one innovation often provokes or is provoked by another. This is not surprising, since organizations are complex entities with many linkages. It may be difficult to discern clearly the boundary between one innovation and the next. Second, innovation should be viewed as a 'state-of-being' for an organization, not as a one-off event.

Reflect: Think of a recent innovation or change in your information organization. Can you identify any other innovations or changes (managed or otherwise) that were provoked by the first innovation?

2.3 Nature or degree of an innovation

Innovations vary considerably in their scale, and associated resource implications and strategic impact. They also vary in the time period over which they are implemented. One way of categorizing innovations is on the basis of their level or degree of newness or novelty. On this basis there are two key terms that are used to differentiate innovation: *radical* and *incremental*.

A *radical innovation* is a 'fundamental change' (Dewar and Dutton, 1986) innovation, often implemented through a specific project; it is typically associated with the development of a new product or service. Depending on the significance of the new product or service, a radical innovation may impact on organizational culture, structure, resource allocation and job roles.

Radical innovations are more likely to emerge from a planned programme of research and development and, as such, are often described as technology-push innovations. Radical innovations are usually associated with high levels of risk because they may present challenges in operationalization, implementation and adoption. They typically involve the development and application of new technology, and may impact on existing market structures and business models. In addition, they are likely to generate opportunities for follow-up innovations as adopters start to experiment with how they want to make use of the innovation, and businesses develop an understanding of the scope for enhancements. For example, the outsourcing of London Borough of Hounslow's library and cultural services to the private sector organization JLIS involved a range of other innovations including the introduction of new human resources expertise and management, new IT infrastructure, new performance systems, new financial systems, restructuring and upskilling of the workforce and library refurbishment (Griffiths and Grier, 2009).

An *incremental innovation* is an add-on to a previous innovation without changing its essential concept (Dewar and Dutton, 1986). Incremental innovation could, for example, take the form of changing the materials used to make a product, improving the product through an updated design, or adding additional features or options. In the service context, such innovation is often a response to information gathered through the regular cycles of feedback embedded in quality auditing and monitoring mechanisms, such as citizen surveys, or student satisfaction surveys. It may also be triggered by a range of external factors, such as the release of a new version of a software suite that is key to the information organization's processes and service delivery, or the release of an upgrade of a library management system. Li (2006), for example, describes a host of relatively minor but useful incremental innovations at Cornell Library. These include the loan of laptop computers and the delivery of books to faculty offices; all improvements are designed to enhance the appropriateness and convenience of the service to users.

This categorization is useful in reflecting the scale of an innovation, but it is necessary to recognize that such descriptors are relative to context. What may be a radical innovation to one organization, or even within an organization to one group, may be viewed as incremental in another organization or to another group in the same organization. Some innovations are difficult to classify as either radical or incremental. For example, the Book Myne App for iPhone users, which locates nearby libraries and allows users to search their catalogues, may be viewed as a minor improvement in catalogue access, or may be found to have significant consequences for catalogue searching, especially when linked with the increasing digitization of information and cultural resources. In addition, radical innovations can have different levels of newness. An innovation may be new to the organization (in which case they may be able to learn from others who have already implemented it) or new-to-the-world, making the producer first to the market and giving potential for market leadership.

The decision to generate radical or incremental innovations depends on the external environment, internal capabilities, budget, resource capability and, most importantly, an organization's engagement with innovation and its willingness to take risks.

Reflect: Identify one incremental and one radical innovation with which you have been involved. What was the innovation process associated with each innovation?

'Radical' and 'incremental' are terms that are used to denote the degree of change a new innovation brings to an organization. However, an innovation may also be differentiated by the level of change that it brings to a sector. *Discontinuous* or *disruptive innovations* are those innovations that bring a significant level of change, not just to an organization, but to a whole industry. They often appear together with major technological changes. Once developed they change the industry and the resources, knowledge and expertise required for success (Anderson and Tushman, 1991). Disruptive innovations require different business models for success, but the structure of the marketplace may change slowly. For example, many eventually disruptive innovations are initially inadequate to the jobs performed by current solutions. Mobile phone technology is a good example. When mobile phones were first used their call quality meant that they had limited application, but as call quality improved they became more of a threat to existing landline services. By the time that the threat was evident, incumbent landline providers found it difficult to catch up. Some potentially disruptive innovations that have been recently launched are Google Apps for Education (www.google.com), a free alternative to Microsoft Office, the University of the People, an 'open' and free university (www.uopeople.org), and handheld educational applications.

The merger of the libraries of a number of law firms could be viewed as a more modest example of a potentially disruptive innovation in the provision of legal information sources. Such a merger would allow law firms to share the costs of access to expensive digital resources while also being able to draw on a wider pool of expertise. However, if such arrangements became the norm, there are potential consequences for careers and expertise as well as for the viability of legal database providers.

Reflect: Identify one information technology innovation that you would describe as a discontinuous innovation because of the effect that it has had throughout the information industry. Discuss the consequences and impacts for different types of stakeholders (organizations and individuals).

2.4 Types of innovation

In addition to classification on the basis of their newness, innovations can be categorized into types on the basis of their outcomes. On this basis it is possible to identify a variety of different types of innovation. Two broad groups are external/tangible and internal/intangible. *External innovations* are those in which customers directly use or benefit from the innovation. Product and service innovations are types of external innovation. *Internal innovations* focus on enhancements in internal processes, such as production systems, ordering and acquisition systems and team working logistics. Customers benefit from such internal innovations indirectly either because they support enhanced service delivery or because they perhaps reduce the cost of a product or service. To survive and prosper, organizations need to invest in a range of different types of innovations, because each type of innovation influences an organization in a different way and achieves different outcomes and impacts (Siguaw, Simpson and Enz, 2006).

Taking this one step further, there is increasing recognition that organizations need to engage in a number of different types of innovation simultaneously, and that, in particular, focusing on just one type of innovation can be detrimental to performance. Indeed, organizations often have no option but to innovate in a number of directions at the same time. For example, to improve their performance, an organization might bring in new equipment or use a new technology which can also be used to add another product to their product range, or, in developing a new product or service, they typically have no choice but to make process innovations. Indeed, the creation of a new learning resource centre building may have consequences for the range of services offered (external innovation) and the processes needed to make sure that those services are available (internal innovation). Unfortunately, all too often the focus is on the external innovation, without sufficient attention being directed towards the associated internal innovation. Kelley and Littman (2006) suggest that organizations need to innovate at 'every point of the compass':

A great product can be one important element in the formula for business success, but companies that want to succeed in today's competitive environment need much more, they need innovation at every point of the compass, in all aspects of the business and among every team member. Building an environment fully engaged in positive change, and a culture rich in creativity and renewal, means creating a company with 360 degrees of innovation.

(Kelley and Littman, 2006, 6)

Over the years there have been many proposals for labels for types of innovation. Here we introduce two of the binary typologies that have been widely used for a long time, and a third typology that is relatively recent, but which offers an interesting strategic perspective. Together these three models offer different approaches for thinking about the types of innovation in organizations. There are overlaps between the models, so, in practice, an organization might want to select a model which best suits its strategic aims and context. Based on a recent study, these typologies are:

- product/service and process innovations
- administrative and technical innovations
- product, process, position and paradigm innovations.

(Baregheh, Rowley and Sambrook, 2011)

2.4.1 Product/service and process innovation

This is one binary categorization of types of innovation. In this typology, innovations are classed either as product innovations or as process innovations (Knight, 1967; Utterback, 1971). Product innovation is concerned with the development of new products and services for the market (customers) while process innovation relates to ways of undertaking production or service operations. Product innovations aim to present a new or improved product or service for the customers, and customers will see the impact of such an innovation in the products or services that they receive, while process innovations change or improve the way that organizations perform and the way in which products and services are created and delivered. Recent examples of service innovations in public libraries, for example, include a library service for immigrant workers, and a teens reading website. A process innovation might be the implementation of a customer satisfaction survey, the introduction of self-service issue, or the implementation of new metadata rules for audio digital objects.

The boundary between product and process innovation is often blurred, and this is especially the case for many service innovations. In the context of service innovation, it is helpful to think of process innovations as being 'back office' (processes that the customers do not see or interact with directly), and to regard service innovations as being 'front office' (processes in which interaction with the customer occurs). For example, offering access to an increasing range of digital content requires the development of expertise in and systems for digital rights management. Esposito (2006) emphasizes the need for libraries to integrate their processes in order to optimize service delivery. He suggests that if the American retail corporation Wal-Mart (now branded Walmart) ran a library, there would be fewer libraries, but they would be much, much bigger. Wal-Mart would study the entire supply chain from authors to readers in order to eliminate inefficiencies. All savings brought about by reconfiguring the supply chain would be passed on to the library's users.

2.4.2 Administrative and technical innovation

This is another (arguably overlapping) binary typology of types of innovation; innovations can be classed as either administrative or technical. Technical innovation relates to new products, processes or services, while an administrative innovation involves changes to the social structure of the organization (such as organizational policies associated with recruitment, the allocation of resources, the structuring of tasks, authority and reward) (Daft, 1978; Evan, 1966).

The term 'technical innovation' is a little wider in scope than might be anticipated. It refers to any type of innovation structured from a technical viewpoint, which lies at the heart of operations and influences the flow of product or process operations (Damanpour, 1991). Technical innovation may take a number of different forms. Bantel and Jackson (1989) suggest:

> Technical innovations pertain to products and services as well as production processes and operations related to the central activities of the organization (design and delivery of products, services, marketing, and office operations); such innovations are assumed to be originated in the technical core of the organization.
>
> (Bantel and Jackson, 1989, 108)

Another widely used term that is difficult to disentangle from technical innovation is 'technological innovation'. Technological innovations are those innovations solely initiated by use of technology, and often provoked by technological advancements. These days many 'technical innovations' or innovations associated with operations and processes involve either information or other technologies, so these two types of innovation are in practice tightly coupled, but it is important to recognize that not all technical innovations involve technology (Damanpour and Evan, 1984).

Administrative innovation brings change to the structure or administration of the organization. Bantel and Jackson perceive administrative innovations as pertaining to:

> change in the organizational structure and the people who populate the organization (staffing, employee survey, strategic planning, compensation system and training programs); these innovations are assumed to originate in the more peripheral, administrative core of the organization.
>
> (Bantel and Jackson, 1989, 108)

Technical innovation is typically associated with a bottom-up approach (an innovation that is initiated by staff at the bottom of the organizational hierarchy and which moves to the upper levels for development) while administrative innovation has a top-down approach (managers decide to adopt or develop an administrative innovation and then staff follow).

Researchers who examined administrative and technical innovation were also interested in the rates of their adoption, and whether adopting one type was typically coupled with the adoption of the other. Evan (1966) believed that the adoption of one type of innovation often provoked the adoption of another type, but that often there was a lag between the adoption of the first and the adoption of the second. He called this the 'organizational lag'. Damanpour and Evan (1984) continued the research on organizational lag based on research in 85 public libraries, and argued the case for the minimization of lag and a balanced adoption of different types of innovation:

> A balanced rate of adoption of administrative and technical innovation is more effective in helping organizations to maintain or improve their level of performance than either administrative or technical innovations alone.
>
> (Damanpour and Evan, 1984, 392)

Ettlie (1988, 2) contributed to the exploration of the relationship between administrative and technical innovation by proposing the concept of *synchronous innovation*, as 'the planned simultaneous adoption of congruent technological and administrative innovations'. He suggested that these two types of innovation work together to create a synergistic effect on performance.

Reflect: Think about the two binary classifications of types of innovation identified above. Which of these approaches would you find the most helpful when trying to understand innovation in your organization?

2.4.3 Product, process, position and paradigm innovations

A more recent and refined classification of types of innovation is that offered by Bessant and Tidd (see also Francis and Bessant); they view innovation from the perspective of the change associated with a specific type of innovation. On this basis they propose the following four categories of innovation:

- *Product innovation*: changes in the things (products/services) which an organization offers.
- *Process innovation*: changes in the way in which things (products/services) are created and delivered.
- *Position innovation*: changes in the context in which products/services are introduced.
- *Paradigm innovation*: changes in the underlying mental models which frame what the organization does.

(Bessant and Tidd, 2007, 13)

Product innovation and process innovation have been discussed above, so here we will focus on position and paradigm innovation.

Position innovation is concerned with the role of innovation in exploiting new customer bases and markets and new ways of offering or introducing the innovation to the potential customer. A position innovation changes the customer's view or understanding of the products (Kim and Mauborgne, 1999). Also 'positional innovation can change the characteristics of a market or create a market that does not exist' (Francis and Bessant, 2005, 175). An example of a position innovation would be an investment in product identity and branding, or seeking and entering a new market for an existing product or service. Information organizations can seek to achieve position innovation, through seeking to reach new groups, enhancing their brand communication, or designing and constructing a new building which through its facilities and design clearly communicates the role of the library going forward.

Paradigm innovation, on the other hand, occurs when the way of looking at things is reframed or simply when the organization changes its business model (revenue generation model). Examples of such innovation would be 'low-cost airlines, the provision of online insurance and other financial services, and the repositioning of drinks like coffee and fruit juice as premium "designer" products' (Tidd, Bessant and Pavitt, 2005, 11). A paradigm innovation requires all of the strategies and principles of the organization to change; a paradigm innovation might entail shifting the product range in a completely new direction or for a new purpose, such as moving to mass production which requires the organization to change its processes, or a joint venture to obtain certain capabilities for a dynamic change. One much quoted example is the transition of the Nokianvirta paper mill to the mobile telephone giant, Nokia. A more topical example is *The Guardian*'s Open Platform Project (www.guardian.co.uk/open-platform). This project illustrates a shift in business model for *The Guardian* from charging for content (as in print newspapers) to free content. The project provides free access to 7,000,000 articles published over the last ten years. The key driver for the project is 'distribution', which can no longer be achieved fully through print newspapers (with a weekday circulation of 400,000), but may be achieved through website hits of 33 million per month.

In summary, position innovation focuses on the adaptation and development of a product for another market or customer group, whereas paradigm innovation is associated with a significant shift in perceptions or markets. Importantly, there are links between these two types of innovations, and both may embed a number of process and product innovations.

Reflect: Position innovations are concerned with changing customers'
perceptions. This might involve significantly changing what the
information organization does, or changing the way that it presents
itself. For example, Leeds Library and Information Services recently
launched a new service to support children with Autistic Spectrum
Disorder (ASD); in doing so they were seeking to change perceptions
of parents regarding the relevance of the library and information

*service in supporting children with ASD. Explain some of the service
and process innovations that might have been necessary in order to
implement a successful position innovation.*

2.5 Information systems and innovation

This section develops further the idea of technological innovation,
mentioned above, with a specific focus on the role of information
systems in innovation within organizations. Many of the
innovations in information organizations are associated with the
availability of new technologies in the marketplace. These new
technologies may either be adopted by information organizations
to make service or process innovations (e.g. a new release of a
library management system), or they may change the market
environment for the organization, such that they need to review
and develop their role, service and position (e.g. online news
services, RFID).

There is widespread acknowledgement that over the past 30 years
information systems have played a significant role in innovation in
all organizations, and information organizations specifically.
Swanson (1994, 1072) defined information systems innovation as:
'Innovation in the organizational application of digital computer
and communication technologies.'

Key information systems for today's organizations are:

- *Enterprise systems* (Enterprise Resource Planning (ERP)
  systems): these integrate and co-ordinate internal business
  processes (for academic journal publishers, the integration of
  manuscript submission and journal production systems).
- *Supply chain management systems*: these maintain effective
  data links and communication with organizations in a supply
  chain (such as, for libraries, the system links that they have
  with book suppliers and journal subscription agents).
- *Customer relationship management systems*: these support the
  integration of customer information from a wide range of

business processes, with a view to enhancing relationships with those customers (for journal subscription agents and journal publishers, systems that collect statistics on journal title use and article downloads under the contracts with different libraries).

Over the last 30 years, organizations have typically experienced several cycles of innovation that involve information systems. This is a continuing process, as new opportunities are presented by new information technology products or services, and new challenges present themselves in changing marketplaces. The challenge lies in maintaining an ongoing effort to identify how information systems can support organizational processes.

An additional perspective on IS innovation is offered by two models which examine technology innovation life cycles. One such model, the Industrial Lifecycle Model, proposed by Utterback and Abernathy (1975), also shows the links between the adoption of a new technology across the industry, and the relative significance of product and process innovation, and radical and incremental innovation at the different stages. The stages are:

1 *Unco-ordinated*: this stage is when a new technology is introduced and the market faces expansion by all those companies that want to adopt it and create competitive improvements; this typically leads to frequent changes to products and to product diversity. At this stage, the rate of radical product innovations is higher than for any other type of innovation.

2 *Segmental*: this stage begins when the new technology has been widely adopted and used in the industry, and hence it is maturing. The focus shifts to price competition, which requires a focus on production processes and quantity production. So at this stage the rate of radical process innovation increases.

3 *Systematic*: at this stage the product has matured and various processes are established, adopted and integrated. Not much

radical change is introduced due to the huge cost of changing the developed operations, and the focus is mainly on incremental product and process innovation. Eventually, introduction of a new technology or changes in market interest lead to the start of another life cycle.

Interestingly, Baras (1990) suggests that models such as the one described above are not applicable to service industry innovations. He goes further and suggests that life cycles for technology-based service innovations are the reverse of those for product innovations. Hence, he refers to his model as the reverse product life cycle. This model has three stages:

1 *Improved efficiency*: after introduction of a new technology organizations tend to apply the new technology to achieve incremental process innovations to improve their efficiency; in this stage organizations are still learning about the new technology and exploiting it.
2 *Improved quality*: as the organizations learn more about the new technology and gain more experience with it, they move towards achieving radical process innovation in order to improve the quality of their service which leads to standardizing procedures and systems.
3 *New products*: at this stage organizations are experienced with the new technology and become engaged in expansion through the new technology by developing radical new services in response to market demand.

Reflect: Think of an example of a technology innovation that has affected the information industry (e.g. Amazon.com, a new metadata standard, Web 2.0 tools). Which of the above two life cycle models would be most useful in profiling the innovations associated with the technology, and why?

2.6 Innovation orientation

While entrepreneurial, innovative and creative individuals are important catalysts for innovation, successful organizations need to 'know' how to innovate. That is, innovation, change and creativity need to be part of the organizational culture and strategy, innovation being valued and rewarded, and forming 'a way of life', everybody constantly asking 'How can we do things better?', and seeking ways to improve. As we have discussed, there are a wide range of different types of innovations, some of which are small scale improvements (incremental innovations) that can be implemented with limited, or possibly no, additional resources other than an inventive mind and a willingness to change. Others involve considerable planning, affect many people, and may take years to implement fully. An organization that is a fertile ground for all types of innovation is described as 'innovation oriented' and is said to have an 'innovation orientation'. Innovation orientation is defined as:

> A multidimensional knowledge structure composed of a learning philosophy, strategic direction, and transfunctional beliefs that, in turn, guide and direct all organizational strategies and actions, including those embedded in the formal and informal systems, behaviours, competencies and processes of the firm to promote innovative thinking and facilitate successful development, evolution, and execution of innovations.
>
> (Siguaw, Simpson and Enz, 2006, 560)

Figure 2.1 is an illustration of the drivers, actions and outcomes of innovation orientation. This shows that innovation orientation takes shape within the learning philosophy, strategic direction and transfunctional acclimation of the organization; these in turn affect organizational competencies, innovation outcomes and firm performance. None of the components in the model in Figure 2.1 just happen. They require strategic leadership and management. Innovative organizations do not just wait for innovation to happen; they have culture and structures that encourage innovation, creativity and entrepreneurship, and processes and systems to

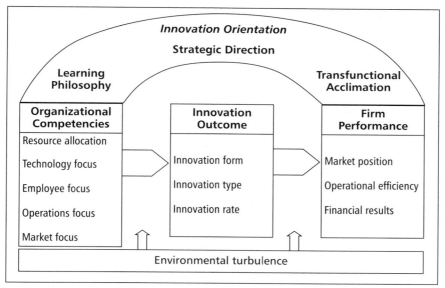

Figure 2.1 *Model of innovation orientation (Siguaw, Simpson and Enz, 2006, 561)*

convert ideas into marketable products and services. Siguaw, Simpson and Enz (2006) suggest that for organizations to adopt an innovation orientation approach they must pay attention to, value and invest in the attitudes and activities listed in Figure 2.2.

1 Creation, development and implementation of innovations should be encouraged and valued within all divisions of the organization.
2 New technologies should be valued, developed and deployed by the organization.
3 Employees at all ranks and levels – especially innovative employees – should be encouraged and motivated.
4 Information on customers, consumers and competitors needs to be collected, analysed and used continuously.
5 Operational processes and structures need to be revised, organized and co-ordinated continuously.
6 An innovative organizational culture should be initiated, shaped and sustained.
7 More of both radical and incremental innovations need to be attended to and developed/generated.
8 More innovations in all of the innovation types – marketing, process and administrative innovations – need to be invested in, developed and generated.
9 Innovations need to be undertaken at a faster rate.

Figure 2.2 *Innovation orientation (based on Siguaw, Simpson and Enz, 2006)*

In introducing the concept of innovation orientation we have started to introduce the importance of the organizational context for innovation and entrepreneurship. This is an important theme which is revisited in much more detail in Chapters 4 and 5.

Reflect: Use Figure 2.2 to assess whether an organization known to you has an innovation orientation. You may wish to score each of the areas on a scale of 1 to 5 and possibly to discuss this with colleagues.

2.7 Innovation management

Innovation is not a simple flash of inspiration but an extended and organized process of turning bright ideas into successful realities.

(Bessant and Tidd, 2007, 298)

Innovation is an important but complex process, which is difficult to manage. Nevertheless, innovation consumes considerable resources, involves many people, and has potentially significant consequences for organizations, so innovation cannot just be left to chance – it needs managing. And, some organizations seem to be better at innovation than others, which suggests that a propensity towards successful innovation can be learned and that the innovation process can be honed. Tidd, Bessant and Pavitt (2005) suggest that optimal innovation management routines are not easy to acquire, and that they tend to be specific to individual organizations.

A number of authors have sought to aid understanding of innovation by proposing models of the stages in the innovation process. Each model has a series of stages; typically a stage will include a number of parallel and co-ordinated activities designed to lead to a successful implementation of a new process or service. There is a critical decision point or filter between each stage. So, for example, moving from the Idea stage to the Design stage in Van de Ven, Angle and Pool's (2000) model below, it is necessary to filter the ideas and select those that will go forward to the design stage.

These models are useful for managing, facilitating and controlling the innovation process in an organization. They aid in the planning of resource allocations and the activities and engagement of stakeholders. Nevertheless, like all n-step management models, such models have their limitations. Extracted from the context of a specific organization and innovation, they only give a superficial overview of the innovation process. In addition, many implicitly assume that innovation is project based. Finally any one model may have varying levels of applicability in different circumstances. Depending on the type of innovation (e.g. process or product/service, radical or incremental), the scale of the innovation, the marketplace drivers for speed, and the culture and structure of the organization, the innovation process may involve a different series of stages, which may be executed over varying periods of time.

Three different innovation process models have been selected for inclusion in this section; these illustrate that different commentators share common ground, but approach the idea of the innovation process from slightly different perspectives.

Van de Ven, Angle and Pool (2000) propose a general purpose model of the innovation process which has four stages:

1 *Idea stage:* a problem is recognized, search for a solution is undertaken, alternatives are diagnosed, and a prototype does not yet exist.

2 *Design stage:* an innovation solution or prototype is developed, adapted or adopted and detailed guidelines for actions are established.

3 *Implementation stage:* the innovation is put into action; scale up operations begin. The innovation may be evaluated to decide whether to expand, modify or discontinue it.

4 *Incorporation, or diffusion, routinization or institutionalization:* the innovation is accepted as part of the standard operating procedures and no longer is viewed as an innovation.

(Van de Ven, Angle and Pool, 2000, 63)

Bessant and Tidd (2007) propose an innovation process model that is subtly different from that proposed by Van de Ven, Angle and Pool. Their 'generate-select-implement' model emphasizes the creativity and ideas generation component of innovation. Its three phases are:

1 *Generate* innovation possibilities: scan and search internal (e.g. staff suggestions, research and development investment, customer behaviour or feedback) and external (e.g. new legislation, competitor action, changes in economic conditions) organizational environments to pick up and process signals about potential innovations.
2 Strategically *select* from those options: make a choice on the basis of impact, either competitively or socially, from the set of potential innovation possibilities that the organization will commit resources to.
3 *Implement*: make innovation happen, by growing an idea through various stages of development to final launch. This process involves gathering, co-ordinating and managing resources, including knowledge, people, and time and cost budgets.

The three identified sub-phases of implement are:

• *Acquiring knowledge resources*: the gathering together of technological knowledge both inside the organization (research and development) and beyond the organization (knowledge transfer), and combining them into a product concept or invention.
• *Executing the project*: the sub-phase during which the innovation is developed and prepared for launch. Often this stage is complex and involves contributions from many different people in different roles and with different backgrounds both within the organization and beyond.
• *Launching the innovation*: this sub-phase is concerned with preparing the market into which the innovation will be

launched. Such a market may be other organizations, consumers, or, for process and other internal innovations, the staff of the organization. This sub-phase involves marketing and communication towards creating an awareness of, and interest in, and ultimately a commitment to, the innovation.

Finally, in acknowledgement of the richness of innovation process models in the literature of new product development, a model from this literature is included. Compared with the models offered above this model contextualizes the innovation process in its commercial context, and emphasizes various aspects of the implementation process more specifically. As outlined here, and as often detailed elsewhere in the new product development literature, the emphasis is on a good rather than on a service. Similar stages and considerations apply for services.

1 *Idea generation*: the search for new ideas; these can come from customers, researchers, competitors, employees, other channel members, and management.

2 *Idea screening*: the selection of ideas for further development; a key consideration is whether the idea is compatible with organizational objectives, strategies and resources.

3 *Concept development*: during which an idea is refined from a product idea (a possible product) to a product concept (with the identification of potential target audiences, potential product benefits, and potential consumption patterns). A product concept allows consideration of the positioning of the product in the marketplace, relative to competitive products and brands.

4 *Concept testing*: this involves presenting the product concept to potential customers, and gathering information on their reactions. The closer the presentation of the concept is to the eventual proposed product, the more informative this stage will be.

5 *Marketing strategy development*: following from a successful concept test, the next stage is to develop a preliminary market plan for launching the product into the market. Typically, this will include:

  — the target market's size, structure and behaviour; the planned
    product positioning; and the sales, market share and profit goals
    for the first few years
  — planned price, distribution strategy and marketing budget for
    the first year
  — the long run sales and profit goals, and marketing mix strategy
    over time.
6 *Business analysis*: involving the development of sales, cost and
  profit projections to determine whether they satisfy company
  objectives.
7 *Product development*: the beginning of significant investment in
  the product, including the creation of product prototypes and the
  design of the product. This stage typically involves a research and
  development department, and functional and customer testing.
8 *Market testing*: at this stage the new product is launched into the
  market in order to assess consumer response and to improve the
  accuracy of projections of the market and business potential of the
  product.
9 *Commercialization*: involves contracting full-scale manufacture,
  roll-out into major markets, and advertising and promotion.

(Kotler, 2003)

In conclusion, there are a number of models of the innovation
process, which can be variously applied to different types of
innovation.

*Reflect: Draw a model of the different stages in the innovation process that
might apply for a new process or service in your organization.*

2.8 Innovation diffusion and adoption

No innovation can be a success unless and until it has been adopted
by its intended users or customers. In some cases, especially for
new products or services where there are a limited number of
potential customers and users, such as in Organization-to-
Organization (O2O) environments, or for internal innovations, the

potential users or adopters of an innovation may be involved in the development process; adoption starts before innovation launch. However, in many instances an innovation may have numerous potential customers or users, and while a few of these may be engaged in concept and innovation testing, most do not become aware of the product until after its launch. In such situations, the use or adoption (the decision to become a regular user of an innovation) gradually diffuses through the potential and targeted customer or user group.

Adopters of innovations (especially services and goods) are often considered to go through the following stages:

1 *Awareness*: the consumer becomes aware of the existence of the innovation.
2 *Interest*: the consumer starts to see the possible value of the innovation and seeks further information about it.
3 *Evaluation*: the consumer considers whether to try the innovation, and compares it with other options for achieving the same outcomes or benefits.
4 *Trial*: the consumer continues to explore the innovation, through a trial, which allows them to enhance their estimate of its potential value.
5 *Adoption*: the consumer commits to the innovation and starts making full and regular use of it.

Users or customers need to be taken through these stages. This involves communication, marketing and various other means of persuasion.

Some people are faster to adopt an innovation than others. Rogers' (2003) model classified adopters into five categories on the basis of their 'innovativeness', and suggested that each of the groups had different value orientations:

1 *Innovators*: are venturesome, and keen to try new ideas.

2 *Early adopters*: are guided by respect; as opinion leaders in their communities they adopt new ideas early, but carefully.

3 *Early majority*: are deliberate; they adopt new ideas before the average person.

4 *Late majority*: are sceptical and adopt an innovation only after the majority have tried it.

5 *Laggards*: are tradition-bound and suspicious of change, mix with other tradition-bound people, and adopt an innovation only when it becomes very widely accepted.

Again, such a model flags very important lessons for the information innovator. Not everyone will show initial enthusiasm for a new service, a new technology or a new way of doing things. Also, those few people who are 'innovators' may be willing to try something simply because it is new. It is not until the innovation has penetrated through much of the early adopter and early majority groups that it can be counted as a success. Finally, success in changing processes or systems within an organization may depend on all employees buying into the innovation. So at some stage effort may need to be directed towards persuading or coercing the laggards!

One of the challenges associated with innovation is predicting the rate of acceptance. Certainly different innovations may be adopted at different rates. There are five characteristics of an innovation that affect its rate of adoption:

1 *Relative advantage*: the degree to which the innovation appears to be superior to other options.

2 *Compatibility*: the degree to which the innovation matches the values, priorities and experiences of potential users.

3 *Complexity*: the relative difficulty in using or understanding the innovation – the easier the better!

4 *Divisibility*: the degree to which the innovation can be tried on a limited basis, to build confidence prior to commitment.

5 *Communicability*: the degree to which the beneficial outcomes from use of the innovation can be communicated to others.

These are important considerations. Some products are inherently complex, while others, such as search engines or websites, can be made to appear easier to use, through appropriate design. Some might argue that social networking sites are popular with teenage girls because they give them an opportunity to engage in something that they would like to do anyway (chat to their friends) (compatibility), and that there is a relative advantage over other options, such as text messaging, because of the relatively increased interactivity.

Reflect: When a new technology (e.g. digital cameras, mobile phones, notebook computers) entered the marketplace were you a technology innovator, early adopter, or . . .?

Summary and conclusions

Innovation and creativity are widely recognized to be essential to the successful evolution and survival of organizations. For many years now information organizations have been buffeted by a range of factors in their environment. At the fore are changes associated with information technology which have changed the way in which people communicate and access information, work together, study and spend their leisure time. In response to such drivers, information organizations have been engaging in change and innovation. In many instances such organizations will be engaging in numerous innovations at any one point in time. This chapter has sought to offer some concepts and frameworks to help information professionals make sense of the complexity of innovation in organizational settings. The chapter started with a definition of innovation which outlined a number of different attributes or characteristics of innovation. On this basis the next two sections explored two significant approaches to classifying innovations, on the basis of their level of novelty (e.g. radical or incremental), and on the basis of the outcome of the innovation (e.g. product/service, or process). The concepts of position and paradigm innovation were also introduced.

Later sections in the chapter offered insights into key aspects of innovation in organizations. The first of these sections discussed the role of information systems in innovation, including discussion of technology life cycle models. Next, the concept of innovation orientation was used to introduce the notion that innovation is a process that requires strategic leadership and management. The theme of the organizational context of innovation is important and will be revisited in later chapters. Next, a section on innovation processes offered some insights into the stage models of innovation that can be used in the management of specific innovation processes. Finally, the chapter concluded with a discussion of the diffusion and adoption of innovations.

Review questions

1　Offer a definition of innovation. Explain the key attributes of innovation, and how they provide a framework for classifying different innovations.

2　Explain, with examples, the concepts of radical and incremental innovations. Use examples to demonstrate why both of these types of innovation are necessary to organizations.

3　Discuss, with examples, what is meant by the following terms relating to types of innovation: product innovation, service innovation, administrative innovation, technical innovation and technological innovation.

4　With specific reference to the concepts of position and paradigm innovation, explain how different types of innovation in organizations are interlinked.

5　What is information systems innovation, and how does it relate to different types of innovation?

6　It is suggested that innovation orientation is a precursor to organizational innovation. What do you understand by the concept of innovation orientation?

7　Innovation is often seen as a process with a number of stages. Outline the stages in one model of the innovation process. Briefly identify the limitations of such models.

8   What are the stages in Rogers' (2003) model of the diffusion of innovation?

Challenges

1   Is it realistic to take a systemic approach to integrating and co-ordinating different types of innovation across an organization?

2   How do managers avoid 'strategic drift' as a consequence of a series of incremental innovations over time, and owned by different people?

3   When does an incremental innovation become a radical innovation?

4   Much of the literature on innovation concentrates on product innovation. Are research findings and practice in this area transferable to service and process innovations?

5   Where is the dividing line between a service innovation and the process innovations that support that service innovation (back office–front office)?

6   Does it matter that there are many different classifications for types of innovation?

7   Is 'innovation orientation' just another idealistic management precept? Would it be better just to focus on supporting and promoting a selected number of individuals as 'innovation and ideas people'?

8   What would be a good stage model for a service innovation process?

9   How can the diffusion and adoption of an innovation be optimized?

Group discussion topics
Group discussion topic 1: Radical and incremental innovation

1   In relation to a radical innovation that you have been involved with in the past two years, briefly explain the nature of the innovation, its rationale, its effects and its benefits.

2   Make a list of a few incremental innovations that you have been involved with in the past two years. *Selecting one* of these incremental innovations, explain why it was important.

Group discussion topic 2: Innovation orientation

1   Take a look at Siguaw, Simpson and Enz's (2006) checklist of innovation orientation indicators and discuss where you think your organization's strengths and weaknesses lie.

Group discussion topic 3: Innovation management

1   Selecting a specific recent innovation please discuss:
   • the stages in the innovation process
   • the participants and their roles at each stage
   • the outcome from each stage.

References and additional reading

Anderson, P. and Tushman, M. L. (1991) Managing through Cycles of Technological Innovation, *Research and Technology Management*, **34** (3), 26–31.

Bantel, K. A. and Jackson, S. E. (1989) Top Management and Innovations in Banking: does the competition of the top team make a difference?, *Strategic Management Journal*, **10** (S1), 107–24.

Baregheh, A., Rowley, J. and Sambrook, S. (2009) Towards a Multidisciplinary Definition of Innovation, *Management Decision*, **47** (8), 1323–39.

Baregheh, A., Rowley, J. and Sambrook, S. (2011) Towards an Innovation-Type Mapping, *Management Decision*, **49** (1), forthcoming.

Barras, R. (1990) Interactive Innovation in Financial Business Services: the vanguard of the service revolution, *Research Policy*, **19**, 215–37.

Bessant, J. and Tidd, J. (2007) *Innovation and Entrepreneurship*, Wiley.

Christensen, C. M. and Overdorf, M. (2000) Meeting the Challenge of Disruptive Change, *Harvard Business Review*, **78** (2), 67–76.

Daft, R. L. (1978) Dual-Core Model of Organizational Innovation, *Academy of Management Journal*, **21** (2), 193–210.

Damanpour, F. (1991) Organizational Innovation: a meta-analysis of effects of determinants and moderators, *Academy of Management Journal*, **34** (3), 555–90.

Damanpour, F. (2009) Combinative Effects of Innovation Types and Organizational Performance: a longitudinal study of service organizations, *Journal of Management Studies*, **46** (4), 650–75.

Damanpour, F. and Evan, W. M. (1984) Organizational Innovation and Performance: the problem of 'organizational lag', *Administrative Science Quarterly*, **29** (3), 392–409.

Dewar, R. D. and Dutton, J. E. (1986) The Adoption of Radical and Incremental Innovations: an empirical analysis, *Management Sciences*, **32** (1), 1422–33.

Esposito, J. J. (2006) What if Wal-Mart Ran a Library?, *Journal of Electronic Publishing*, **9** (1), www.journalofelectronicpublishing.org.

Ettlie, J. E. (1988) *Taking Charge of Manufacturing*, Jossey-Bass.

Ettlie, J. E., Bridges, W. and O'Keefe, R. (1984) Organizational Strategy and Structural Differences for Radical versus Incremental Innovations, *Management Science*, **30** (6), 682–95.

Evan, W. M. (1966) Organizational Lag, *Human Organizations*, **25** (1), 51–3.

Francis, D. and Bessant, J. (2005) Targeting Innovation and Implications for Capability Development, *Technovation*, **25** (3), 171–83.

Griffiths, C. and Grier, T. (2009) Managing in the Private Sector, *Library + Information Gazette*, 20 Nov–10 Dec, 1.

Kelley, T. and Littman, J. (2006) *The Ten Faces of Innovation: strategies for heightening creativity*, Profile Books.

Kim, W. C. and Mauborgne, R. (1999) Southwest Airlines' Route to Success, *Financial Times*, May 13, www.ft.com

Knight, K. E. (1967) A Descriptive Model of Intra-Firm Innovation Process, *Journal of Business*, **40** (Oct), 478–96.

Kotler, P. (2003) *Marketing Management*, 11th edn, Prentice Hall.

Li, X. (2006) Library as Incubating Space for Innovations: practices, trends and skill sets, *Library Management*, **27** (6/7), 370–8.

McAdam, R., Reid, R. and Gibson, D. (2004) Innovation and Organisational Size in Irish SMEs: an empirical study, *International Journal of Innovation Management*, **8** (2), 147–65.

Rogers, E. M. (2003) *Diffusion of Innovations*, 4th edn, Simon and Schuster.

Siguaw, J. A., Simpson, P. M. and Enz, C. A. (2006) Conceptualizing Innovation Orientation: a framework for study and integration of innovation research, *Journal of Product Innovation Management*, **23** (6), 556–74.

Swanson, E. B. (1994) Information Systems Innovation among Organizations, *Management Science*, **40** (9), 1069–92.

Tang, H. K. (1998) An Integrative Model of Innovation in Organizations, *Technovation*, **18** (5), 297–309.

Tidd, J., Bessant, J. and Pavitt, K. (2005) *Managing Innovation: integrating technological, market and organizational change*, Wiley.

Utterback, J. M. (1971) The Process of Technological Innovation within the Firm, *Academy of Management Journal*, **14** (1), 75–88.

Utterback, J. M. and Abernathy, W. J. (1975) A Dynamic Model of Process and Product Innovation, *The International Journal of Management Science*, **3** (6), 639–56.

Van de Ven, A. H., Angle, H. L. and Pool, M. S. (2000) *Research on the Management of Innovation: The Minnesota Studies*, Oxford University Press.

3

Entrepreneurship
Co-authored by Siwan Mitchelmore

Learning objectives

After reading this chapter you should be able to:

- Understand the development of the concept of entrepreneurship.
- Discuss what it means to be an entrepreneur and consider your role as an entrepreneur.
- Understand the unique characteristics of public entrepreneurship and their implications for information organizations.
- Reflect on the relevance of social entrepreneurship to information organizations.
- Appreciate the value of entrepreneurial competencies.

3.1 Introduction

The concept of entrepreneurship was introduced in Chapter 1. In this context we emphasized the concept of opportunity-centred entrepreneurship, and the links between innovation and entrepreneurship. The stance taken in this book is that entrepreneurship is the process by which individuals pursue opportunities without regard to the resources they currently control. The essence of entrepreneurial behaviour is identifying opportunities, and converting them into useful outcomes. Such perspectives are important and useful in understanding the relevance of entrepreneurship to a wide range of organizational settings, and offer preliminary insights into entrepreneurial behaviour. This chapter develops the theme of entrepreneurship further by taking an excursion around some of the ideas in the entrepreneurship literature that are likely to be the most helpful to information practitioners or aspiring information entrepreneurs. The objective of the chapter is to provide some concepts and frameworks to support entrepreneurs in developing their aspirations to make a difference into sustained, productive and effective entrepreneurial behaviour.

This chapter commences with a discussion of the development of the concept of entrepreneurship and, most specifically, its roots in commercial enterprises in which entrepreneurship is associated with the creation of new ventures, and the generation of profit. This is followed by a consideration of what it means to be an entrepreneur, and entrepreneurial characteristics, traits and behaviours. Next, there is an exploration of the contextual nature of entrepreneurship by developing discussion of public sector corporate entrepreneurship and social entrepreneurship, respectively. These two types of entrepreneurship offer the most useful insights into the practice of entrepreneurship for the information professional. Finally, the focus shifts to a discussion of entrepreneurial competencies, those competencies that are key to successful entrepreneurship.

3.2 The origins of the concept of entrepreneurship

The word 'entrepreneur' derives from the French words *entre* meaning 'between' and *prendre* meaning 'to take'. The word was originally used to describe people who 'take on the risk' between buyers and sellers or who 'undertake' a task, such as starting a new venture. Early contributions from authors such as Cantillon (1755) regarded the entrepreneur as a person who would make buying and selling decisions in changing market conditions in the search for profit opportunities, buying in one place at a known present price and selling elsewhere at an unknown future value. This context has led to a strong economic tradition in the theory of entrepreneurship. The entrepreneur has been seen as an agent of economic change and activity and has been linked with various functions such as those of capitalist, co-ordinator of limited resources, innovator and risk-taker (Schumpeter, 1934; Knight, 1961; Kirzner, 1973).

Over the years since the mid-18th century there have been contributions to the theory of entrepreneurship from the French, British, German, Austrian and American schools of thought, each with their different emphases on the notion of entrepreneurship and the entrepreneur. Herbert and Link (1982) distilled these various perspectives into a taxonomy of definitions of entrepreneurship theories with 12 distinct themes (as shown in Table 3.1). They make an important differentiation between static and dynamic or processual definitions. In static definitions, none of creativity, change or uncertainty is involved, and the entrepreneur is seen as playing a fixed role in economic exchanges. In processual/dynamic theories, where uncertainty is assumed to exist, the emphasis is on the entrepreneur's role in creating or exploiting innovations and profit opportunities. Binks and Vale (1990) suggested that there were three main theoretical perspectives on the role of the entrepreneur:

1 the innovative entrepreneur causing economic change
   (Schumpeter)
2 the reactive entrepreneur as an agent of adjustment in the
   market economy (Kirzner)
3 the entrepreneur causing incremental, gradual change through
   management of the enterprise (Leibenstein).

Kirzner sees the entrepreneur as being motivated by profit in a market environment, and continuously searching for new opportunities. The success of the entrepreneur is dependent on a superior ability to perceive and act on opportunities, as a result of being able to learn from experience faster and more effectively than competitors. Kirzner offered a tactical, short-term and stree wise understanding of entrepreneurial behaviour. In contrast Schumpeter, often seen as one of the main thinkers in modern entrepreneurship theory, took a more strategic perspective. Schumpeter suggested that the entrepreneur sees possibilities for new solutions unrecognized by others and innovates through making 'new combinations' which make existing products obsolete and which change the economic context of the market (Rae, 2007). Schumpeter saw the entrepreneur as an innovator who engages in a process of creative destruction by disrupting the flow of the market economics of production and consumption, which tends towards price equilibrium, by initiating new products and processes to replace existing offerings and firms which, in turn, became marginal or uncompetitive. He saw the entrepreneur as an innovator, rather than a profit seeker, and as an initiator of change, who also needed to be a manager and a leader, and to undertake 'learning in his [*sic*] natural and social world so that actions can be simply and reliably calculated' (Schumpeter, 1934, 121).

Table 3.1 *Taxonomy of themes in entrepreneurial theory (Herbert and Link, 1982)*	
Themes in static definitions of entrepreneur	**Themes in dynamic/processual definitions of entrepreneur**
The person who supplies financial capital. A manager or superintendent. The owner of an enterprise. An employer of factors of production.	Risk-taking. Innovating. Decision-making. Leading an industry. Organizing economic resources. Contracting. Arbitrage (market-maker). Allocating resources.

In summary, entrepreneurship, and the new ventures that it creates, are essential components of any economic system. This has led to a focus on the role of the entrepreneur as an agent in economic systems. However, to advance a notion of entrepreneurship that embraces commercial, corporate and social entrepreneurship, it is more fruitful to view entrepreneurship as a set of processes and behaviours, a way of working which is contingent and flexible. Not only is such an approach accommodating of different 'types' of entrepreneurship, but it also invites consideration of entrepreneurial behaviour as a matter of degree, such that a person is not either an entrepreneur or not, but that they may exhibit degrees of entrepreneurial behaviour, and that they may, for example, vary in the extent to which they engage in creating or taking advantage of opportunities at different times and in different contexts.

Reflect: Identify a context or time when you were <u>not</u> being entrepreneurial (i.e. not seeking opportunities to do things differently). Why not? Was this the right thing to do at the time?

3.3 Being an entrepreneur

The experience of being an entrepreneur is increasingly being explored as a human, social, behavioural and cultural phenomenon, in pursuit of an understanding of entrepreneurial activity in the social world. Early researchers focused to a great extent on the search for an entrepreneurial personality to help in defining and characterizing an entrepreneur, in order to be able to identify those individuals with the greatest propensity towards entrepreneurial behaviour. As discussed above, more recent theories argue for a more flexible and contingent approach, propose that entrepreneurial behaviour is learned, and therefore focus on the processes that facilitate such learning. This perspective is consistent with the concept of entrepreneurial competencies, which will be discussed in due course in Section 3.6. However, first we explore the more traditional perspective on being an entrepreneur, through considering the characteristics, traits, attributes, behaviours and mindsets of entrepreneurs.

Every textbook on entrepreneurship includes a list of entrepreneurial characteristics or traits. While the very diversity of these lists and the implicit lack of consensus is evidence of the elusiveness of a definition of entrepreneurship, such lists are attractive for their simplicity and as a reflection of perspectives that can be adopted on the nature of entrepreneurship and entrepreneurial behaviours. If personality traits could be identified and categorized, this would enable behaviour to be explained and predicted. Such lists of traits and behaviours do not, however, say anything about how people actually learn and work in entrepreneurial ways.

Early researchers focused their search on a single personality trait that could be associated with entrepreneurial behaviour. This single trait approach explored, variously, a need for achievement, an internal locus of control, a need for autonomy, and a propensity towards risk taking as personality traits that predisposed individuals to entrepreneurial behaviours:

- *Need for achievement* (n-Ach): refers to the drive to excel, to achieve a goal and to be successful (McClelland, 1961).
- *Internal locus of control*: relates to the individual's belief in the extent to which the outcome(s) of an event/action is contingent on their behaviour rather than being the result of external forces such as other people or organizations.
- *Need for autonomy* (n-Aut): relates to an individual's desire for independence, and is related to the perception of entrepreneurs as 'loners' and anti-authority figures who are uncomfortable with structure and dislike constraints on their freedom of action.
- *Risk-taking propensity*: early theories of entrepreneurship emphasize the link between risk taking and entrepreneurship. However, there is a general consensus that the entrepreneur is a risk manager, rather than a risk taker; they exercise good judgement in assessing the risk, and take a decision that will tend to maximize positive outcomes if successful and minimize negative outcomes if unsuccessful.

Reflect: McClelland (1961) suggested that individuals with a high n-Ach tended to have the following attributes:

- *A preference for personal risks and a willingness to work harder in such situations.*

- *A belief that one's personal efforts will be influential in the attainment of some goal and pleasure derived from this belief.*
- *A tendency to perceive the probability of success in attaining a goal as being relatively high.*
- *A need for feedback regarding success or failure of their efforts.*
- *The capacity to plan ahead and to be particularly aware of the passage of time.*
- *An interest in excellence for its own sake.*

On a scale of 1 to 5 (1=low, 5=high) score yourself on each of these attributes.

More recent commentators have abandoned the search for the single defining trait associated with entrepreneurship, and have, instead, generated lists of such traits or characteristics. Table 3.2 shows two such lists which are illustrative of those in the literature. Further lists specific to corporate and social entrepreneurs are offered in the next section.

More recently there has been a trend towards discussing entrepreneurship in terms of entrepreneurial behaviours. Figure 3.1 shows a summary of such a list, based on discussion of the entrepreneurial mindset (McGrath and MacMillan, 2000). It can sometimes be difficult to differentiate between a list of entrepreneurial characteristics and a list of entrepreneurial behaviours. For example, is 'a networker' a characteristic or a behaviour? Further examples of entrepreneurial behaviours are noted and discussed in the following sections on corporate and social entrepreneurship.

Reflect: *Think of someone who you would describe as entrepreneurial. Which of the traits listed in Table 3.2 could be used to describe them?*
How many of the traits in Table 3.2 do you think should be applicable to a person before you describe them as an entrepreneur?

Table 3.2 *Exemplar lists of entrepreneurial attributes/traits*

Entrepreneurial attributes (Gibb, 1993)	Common traits and characteristics of entrepreneurs (Barringer and Ireland, 2008)
Initiative.	Achievement motivated.
Strong persuasive powers.	Alert to opportunities.
Moderate rather than high risk-taking ability.	Creative.
Flexibility.	Decisive.
Creativity.	Energetic.
Independence/Autonomy.	Has a strong work ethic.
Problem-solving ability.	Is a moderate risk taker.
Need for achievement.	Is a networker.
Imagination.	Lengthy attention span.
High belief in control of one's destiny.	Optimistic disposition.
Leadership.	Persuasive.
Hard work.	Promoter.
	Resource assembler/leverager.
	Self-confident.
	Self-starter.
	Tenacious.
	Tolerant of ambiguity.
	Visionary.

Entrepreneurs share the following characteristics:

1 They passionately seek new opportunities and are always looking for the chance to profit from change and disruption in the way that business is done.
2 They pursue opportunities with enormous discipline. Habitual entrepreneurs not only spot opportunities but they make sure that they act on them.
3 They pursue only the very best opportunities, and they avoid exhausting themselves and their organizations by chasing after every option.
4 They focus on execution – specifically adaptive execution . . . they move forward rather than analysing new ideas to death.
5 They engage the energies of everyone in their domain. They create and sustain networks of relationships rather than going it alone, making the most of the intellectual and other resources that people have to offer, all the while helping those people to achieve their goals as well.

Figure 3.1 *The entrepreneurial mindset (McGrath and MacMillan, 2000, based on Kaplan and Warren, 2007, 13–14)*

In conclusion, a number of traits or characteristics have been proposed as a means of identifying an entrepreneur and understanding entrepreneurial behaviour. However, although there is some agreement on the relevance of some characteristics, there is no overall consensus. Cultural, family and economic circumstances may lead to the prioritization of different characteristics in different contexts, and affect the propensity to engage in entrepreneurship. In addition, many of the characteristics and behaviours of entrepreneurs are also shared by successful managers and leaders in other contexts, suggesting that enterprising behaviour is relevant in many 'walks of life', as discussed in greater detail in the next two sections. There is also a growing school of thought that argues that enterprising behaviour and activity is not an inherent characteristic of an individual, but can be learned. Rae (2007, 29) suggests that 'enterprising activity can be learned', but that 'differences in ability are likely to lead to differing outcomes in achievement'.

The final section in this chapter takes up this theme by considering entrepreneurial competencies, the competencies (knowledge, skills and behaviours) that entrepreneurs learn and develop.

3.4 Public sector corporate entrepreneurship

This section discusses the nature and experience of corporate entrepreneurship as applied in the context of public sector organizations. This topic is discussed in some detail here because many information professionals work in libraries that are in the public sector and which are involved in collaborative innovation with other public sector organizations and agencies. Public sector corporate entrepreneurship has two key features. First, the entrepreneurship takes place within a large organization, i.e. it is corporate. Second, that organization is in the public sector, i.e. it is public sector based. Both of these features have a significant impact on how libraries as organizations and information professionals, as individuals, engage in entrepreneurship and innovation. Commentators have discussed variously the dimensions or key characteristics of corporate entrepreneurship, the differences in different sectoral contexts, and the specific challenges facing public sector entrepreneurs.

3.4.1 What is corporate entrepreneurship?

Corporate entrepreneurship is concerned with entrepreneurship within an established and typically (but not always) large organization. The terms 'intrapreneurship' and 'corporate entrepreneurship' can be used interchangeably and this is the approach adopted in this book. However, some authors, such as Antoncic and Hisrich (2003), make a distinction between the terms on the basis that corporate entrepreneurship implies large firms, whereas intrapreneurship can be applied in a wider range of organizational contexts.

Corporate entrepreneurship, in common with entrepreneurship in general, is considered to be both an individual level and an organizational level phenomenon. So, for example, for an academic library there are potentially at least three levels at which corporate entrepreneurship can operate and be discussed – at the level of individual staff, at the level of the academic library, and at the level of the university of which the library is part. Optimally, there should be a commitment to and engagement with entrepreneurship at all levels. Both an organizational environment that encourages entrepreneurship and individuals who are committed and inspired to act entrepreneurially are necessary to successful entrepreneurship and innovation.

At the individual level, corporate entrepreneurship refers to the actions and behaviours of the individual corporate entrepreneur, or innovation agent. This is discussed further in Section 3.4.2.

At the organizational level, corporate entrepreneurship is associated with those processes, behaviours and activities that are managed and developed in order to engender entrepreneurial behaviour within an established organization, enhance organizational entrepreneurial competencies and develop opportunities for innovation. For example, Hayton and Kelley (2006, 407) offer the following definition of corporate entrepreneurship: 'corporate entrepreneurship is a set of firm wide activities that centres on the discovery and pursuit of new opportunities through innovation, new business creation, or the introduction of new business models'.

Antoncic and Hisrich (2003) see intrapreneurship as referring to emergent behavioural intentions and behaviours that are related to departures from the customary ways of doing business in existing organizations. They propose that intrapreneurship is a multi-dimensional concept with eight related components, those being: new ventures, new businesses, product/service innovativeness, process innovativeness, self-renewal, risk taking, proactiveness and competitive aggressiveness, as shown in Table 3.3. They, then, view innovativeness as one aspect of intrapreneurship, supported by other dimensions that are often associated with innovation, such as risk taking and proactiveness.

Table 3.3 *Intrapreneurship dimensions (based on Antoncic and Hisrich, 2003)*

Dimension	Definition
New ventures	Creation of new autonomous or semi-autonomous units or firms.
New businesses	Pursuit of, and entering into, new businesses related to current products or markets.
Product/service innovativeness	Creation of new products and services.
Process innovativeness	Innovation in production procedures and techniques.
Self-renewal	Strategy reformation, reorganization and organizational change.
Risk taking	Possibility of loss relating to quickness in taking bold actions and committing resources in the pursuit of new opportunities.
Proactiveness	Top management orientation for pioneering and initiative taking.
Competitive aggressiveness	Aggressive posturing towards competitors.

Reflect: Review the intrapreneurship dimensions in Table 3.3. Rate your information organization on each of these dimensions, comparing it with other information organizations in the same sector, using a 5-point scale (5 = very high, 1= very low).

Corporate entrepreneurship, in general, is seen to be important to organizational renewal, growth, wealth creation, competitive advantage and positioning in the marketplace, and the generation of new employment opportunities. Organizations may engage in internal innovation in order to introduce new products or services or to enter new markets; they may change their internal processes, structures and capabilities; they may identify and prepare for new ways of competing in existing markets or for entering new markets (Covin and Miles, 1999). Some organizations are more successful at fostering entrepreneurship and innovation and exploiting new opportunities than others. Evidence suggests that the external environment (Covin and Slevin, 1989), organizational culture (Zahra, 1991) and structure (Miller, 1983) are three key factors. Further, as Hayton and Kelley (2006) suggest, and as discussed later in this chapter, the entrepreneurial competencies of individuals within the organization are also important.

3.4.2 The public sector corporate entrepreneur

The recognition that in changing and complex environments all existing organizations need to be effective innovators led to the proposal in the 1980s that entrepreneurship was as important for existing organizations as it was for new enterprises. Commenting in 1987, Luchsinger and Bagby (1987) discuss the difference between an entrepreneur and an intrapreneur. They suggest that the main difference is one of setting. The entrepreneur defines their own setting, while the intrapreneur operates within the setting of an established organization, with structural and procedural constraints. However, both rely heavily on teamwork and group innovation. The intrapreneur is considered to face a greater challenge, due to their lack of control over their environment. On the other hand, the financial risk is carried by the intrapreneur's organization, whereas the entrepreneur bears this risk themselves. Failure means bankruptcy to the entrepreneur, but the intrapreneur can return to the parent organization. The entrepreneur is the boss, while the intrapreneur must still report to superiors and seek sponsorship, and may be subject to internal criticism or resistance. Table 3.4 shows a more recent summary of the differences between private, corporate and public sector entrepreneurs. Notice the differences in objectives and focus, and the effect that the context has on the innovation process, and the approaches to opportunity identification and risk taking. However, perhaps the most important message to be taken from Table 3.4 is that the same dimensions, i.e. objectives, focus, innovation, opportunity and risk taking, are applicable in all cases. Zerbinati and Souitaris (2005)

Table 3.4 *Comparing private, corporate and public sector entrepreneurs (based on Kearney, Hisrich and Roche, 2008) (continued overleaf)*

	Private entrepreneur	Corporate entrepreneur	Public sector entrepreneur
Objectives	Freedom to discover and exploit profitable opportunities; independent and goal orientated; high need for achievement.	Requires freedom and flexibility to pursue projects without being bogged down in bureaucracy; goal orientated; motivated but influenced by corporate characteristics.	Motivated by power and achievement; undertakes purposeful activity to initiate, maintain or aggrandize one or more public sector organizations; not constrained by profit.
Focus	Strong focus on the external environment; competitive environment and technological advancement.	Focus on innovative activities and orientations such as development of new products, services, technologies, administrative techniques, strategies and competitive postures; concentrates on the internal and external environment.	Aims to create value for citizens by bringing together unique combinations of public and/or private resources to exploit social opportunities; learns to use external forces to initiate and achieve internal change.

Table 3.4 *Comparing private, corporate and public sector entrepreneurs (continued)*

	Private entrepreneur	Corporate entrepreneur	Public sector entrepreneur
Innovation	Creates value through innovation and seizing opportunity without regard to resources (human and capital); produces resources or endows existing resources with enhanced potential for creating wealth.	A system that enables and encourages individuals to use creative processes that enable them to apply and invent technologies that can be planned, deliberate, and purposeful in terms of the level of innovative activity desired; instigation of renewal and innovation within that organization.	Public managers are entrepreneurial in the way that they take risks with an opportunistic bias towards action and consciously overcome bureaucratic and political obstacles that their innovations face.
Opportunity	Pursues an opportunity, regardless of the resources they control; relatively unconstrained by situational forces.	Pursues an opportunity independent of the resources they currently control; doing new things and departing from the customary in order to pursue opportunities.	Uses every opportunity to distinguish their public enterprise and leadership style from what is the norm in the public sector; understands the business as well as supporting the opportunity for business growth and development.
Risk taking	Risk taking is a prime factor in the entrepreneurial character and function; assumes significant personal and financial risk, but attempts to minimize them.	Moderate risk taker; recognizes that risks are career related.	Calculated risk taker; takes relatively big organizational risks, but avoids taking big personal risks.

identify three categories of entrepreneurs in the public sector. Table 3.5 summarizes these roles, and their characteristics.

Intrapreneurs can be important nodes of innovation within organizations, provided that the organizational climate supports their creativity, invention and innovation. However, Pinchot (1985),

Table 3.5 *Role of entrepreneurs in the public sector (based on Zerbinati and Souitaris, 2005)*

	Political	Public-social	Community-virtual
Organizational type	Governmental organization.	Non-profit/public/voluntary organization (university, charity, hospital).	Are not in an organization, but rather in a community.
Role and position	Politicians.	Public officers.	Local public figures/regional developers.
Main activity	Create value for citizens by bringing together unique combinations of resources.	Create value for citizens by bringing together unique combinations of resources.	Facilitate and inspire entrepreneurship and renewal within their community.

in his famous 'ten commandments' (Figure 3.2), suggested that too often intrapreneurs are not always smiled upon by managers. Intrapreneurs seek to convert new ideas into actions. In this process they seek to empower others, and draw them into their sphere of influence, let them make their own mistakes, and use these as a vehicle for collective and individual development. More

1 Come to work each day willing to be fired.
2 Circumvent any orders aimed at stopping your dream.
3 Do any job needed to make your project work, regardless of your job description.
4 Find people to help you.
5 Follow your intuition about the people you choose and work only with the best.
6 Work underground as long as you can – publicity triggers the corporate immune system.
7 Never bet on a race unless you are running it.
8 Remember that it is easier to ask for forgiveness than for permission.
9 Be true to your goals and be realistic about the way you achieve them.
10 Keep your sponsors informed.

Figure 3.2 *The intrapreneur's ten commandments (Pinchot, 1985)*

recently, in a study in public sector health and social care organizations, Heinonen and Toivonen (2008) also found that managers are more likely to support 'silent followers' than the corporate entrepreneur who is often self-confident, demonstrates initiative and often critically questions existing working modes.

> *Reflect: Have you ever observed in action someone that you would regard as an intrapreneur? What was the response of managers and others in power to them and their activities? What does this tell you about the organization in which they were working?*

3.4.3 Challenges facing public sector corporate entrepreneurs

Promoting entrepreneurship, and thereby learning how to manage innovation in order to offer new kinds of service and to improve the efficiency of their processes and service delivery, is crucial for all public sector organizations. However, there is a strong school of thought that suggests that there are a number of barriers to innovation in the public sector. These are variously seen to be associated with the lack of competitive pressure to innovate (Borins, 2002a), conflicts with traditional values such as due process and accountability (e.g. Gawthrop, 1999), and that managers in the public sector have lower levels of flexibility than managers in business organizations (Rainey, Backoff and Levin, 1976). In addition, many public sector organizations are large, and highly bureaucratized; they are structured to perform their core tasks with stability and consistency, and to resist change or disruption to these tasks (Wilson, 1989). Finally the incentive to be innovative is often lower in the public sector. Borins (2002a, 468) suggests that 'public sector organizations . . . can be expected to have personnel systems that do not reward career public servants for successful innovation but punish them for unsuccessful attempts'.

Table 3.6 lists some of the barriers to public sector innovation, under the three categories: bureaucracy/organization, political environment

Table 3.6 *Barriers to public sector innovation (based on Borins, 2001)*		
Bureaucracy/Organization	**Political environment**	**External environment**
Hostile attitudes.	Inadequate funding or resources.	Public doubts about the effectiveness of the programme.
Turf fights.	Legislative or regulatory constraints.	Difficulty in reaching the programme's target group.
Difficulty in co-ordinating organizations.	Political opposition.	Opposition by those affected in the private sector.
Logistical problems.		General public opposition or scepticism.
Difficulty in maintaining enthusiasm.		
Difficulty in introducing new technology.		
Union opposition.		
Middle management resistance.		
Opposition to entrepreneurial action.		

and external environment. Of these three sets, Borins (2002b) found that the largest number of obstacles arise in the internal organization and bureaucratic group. This reflects the fact that public sector innovations can impact on operating procedures, power structure and dynamics, and job roles and career prospects. On the other hand, some researchers, most notably Damanpour and Evan (1984) in their seminal study of public libraries, disagree that public sector organizations are less innovative than business organizations. Indeed, Sadler (2000) in his study of corporate entrepreneurship in the public sector demonstrated that the same constraints and stimulants of entrepreneurship applied to both public and private sector organizations, although they may impact differently. Interestingly, he noted that entrepreneurial public sector organizations:

- perceived the environment to be more turbulent than conservative organizations
- tended to have participative decision-making processes and dispersed power bases which foster many innovation-supporting coalitions
- tended to use fewer integrating devices than conservative organizations
- were more autonomous than conservative organizations
- tended to be output focused.

3.5 Social entrepreneurship

As discussed in Chapter 1, social entrepreneurship shares with public entrepreneurship a focus on the creation of 'social value' or 'community value'. Therefore, social entrepreneurship and public entrepreneurship are linked, but social entrepreneurship is not restricted to public sector organizations and, equally importantly, public sector organizations have specific mandates, processes, structures and systems which may constrain their scope for the creation of social value. Therefore, while there is a clear imperative in a rapidly changing public sector for libraries and their staff to engage in public entrepreneurship, their mandate for engagement in social entrepreneurship is less clear. Nevertheless, many libraries and information professionals aspire to 'making a difference', and would benefit from further reflection on the nature of social entrepreneurship.

3.5.1 Defining and understanding social entrepreneurship

The most notable examples of social entrepreneurship involve new non-profit venture creation by individuals with drive and vision, but social entrepreneurship can be conducted within existing non-profit, public sector and business organizations. Libraries engage in social entrepreneurship when they seek and take opportunities to contribute social or community value. Public libraries, in particular, are increasingly defined by the contribution that they make to learning, culture, reading and access to information in order to contribute social value to their communities.

Increasingly, both social enterprises and businesses are concerned with 'more-than-profit', and use blended business value models that combine revenue and profit generation with the generation of social value. Successful social entrepreneurship involves the management of people, capital and other resources in order to capitalize on an opportunity and, as such, significant outcomes can usually only be achieved through an organization or a network of organizations (for further discussion of innovation and networking see Section 5.4). As Austin, Stevenson and Wei-Skillern (2006, 2) suggest: 'We define social entrepreneurship as innovative, social value creating activity that can occur within or across the non-profit, business, or government sectors.'

The stance that social entrepreneurship is not restricted to 'social enterprises' poses difficulties in developing a clear view of the nature of social entrepreneurship and its differentiation from commercial entrepreneurship. Most commentators take the position that the distinction between social and commercial entrepreneurship is not dichotomous, but is more appropriately viewed as a continuum ranging from purely social to purely economic and that it is not possible to fix a boundary between social and commercial entrepreneurship. Taking a pragmatic perspective, Austin, Stevenson and Wei-Skillern (2006) suggest that the central driver for social entrepreneurship is the social problem being addressed, and the particular organizational form that a social enterprise takes should be a decision based on which format would most effectively mobilize the resources needed to address the problem.

Peredo and McLean (2006) suggest that the continuum between social and commercial entrepreneurship can be seen in terms of the relative importance of social goals and commercial exchange to the organization. Table 3.7 shows how they articulate five points on this continuum.

Table 3.7 *The social entrepreneurship continuum (based on Peredo and McLean, 2006, 63)*

High level of social entrepreneurship				Low level of social entrepreneurship
Enterprise goals are exclusively social.	Enterprise goals are exclusively social.	Enterprise goals are chiefly social, but not exclusively.	Social goals are prominent among other goals of the enterprise.	Social goals are among the goals of the enterprise, but subordinate to others.
No commercial exchange.	Some commercial exchange, with any profits directed to social benefit or used to support the enterprise.	Commercial exchange; profits in part to support entre-preneur and/or supporters.	Commercial exchange; profit making for entre-preneur and others is a strong objective.	Commercial exchange; profit making to entrepreneur and others is prominent or prime objective.

Reflect: Where would you place the following organizations on the above spectrum: Tesco, Cancer Research UK, Oxfam, Cooperative Society, your local theatre company, your local public library, a local reading group?

Neck, Brush and Allen (2009) suggest that in delineating and categorizing social entrepreneurship it is not sufficient to consider social mission alone, but it is also important to consider the social impact of an organization. On this basis they propose four categories of entrepreneurial ventures as shown in Figure 3.3. These categories are:

1 *Social purpose ventures*: these are founded on the premise that a social problem will be solved, yet the venture is for-profit and the impact on the market is typically perceived as economic.
2 *Traditional ventures*: these focus primarily on economic mission and economic impact; such ventures have no explicit social mission.

		Venture mission	
		Economic	Social
Primary market impact	Economic	Traditional (2)	Social purpose (1)
	Social	Social consequence (3)	Enterprising nonprofits (4)

Figure 3.3 *Typology of entrepreneurial ventures (based on Neck, Brush and Allen, 2009)*

3 *Social consequence ventures*: these are similar to traditional ventures except that many of their practices have social outcomes; these social outcomes are not the reasons for the firm's existence but rather an outcome of doing business. Such ventures typically associate themselves with corporate social responsibility.

4 *Enterprising nonprofits*: these have earned income activities, and focus on growth and economic sustainability, and may be funded by venture philanthropists.

There are also hybrid organizations that have behaviours and characteristics associated with more than one of the types 1–4. Neck, Brush and Allen (2009) take the position that social entrepreneurship is determined by social mission, and that therefore, although 'social' has a role in three of the four types, only social purpose ventures and enterprising nonprofits fall within the domain of social entrepreneurship. On the other hand, they acknowledge that economic success is an important driver of jobs and wealth, which in turn have social impact. They conclude:

> Entrepreneurship has often been cited as the engine of economic growth . . . . Today, economic growth is still necessary, but no longer sufficient. Social entrepreneurship is the engine of positive, systemic change that will alter what we do, how we do it, and why it matters.
>
> (Neck, Brush and Allen, 2009, 18)

In summary, then, as Peredo and McLean suggest, social entrepreneurship is exercised when some person or group:

1 Aims at creating social value, either exclusively or at least in some prominent way.
2 Shows a capacity to recognize and take advantage of opportunities to create that value.
3 Employs innovation, ranging from outright innovation to adapting someone else's novelty, in creating and/or distributing social value.
4 Is/are willing to accept an above-average degree of risk in creating and disseminating social value.
5 Is/are usually resourceful in being relatively undaunted by scarce assets in pursuing their social venture.

(Peredo and McLean, 2006, based on p. 64)

3.5.2 The social entrepreneur and their challenges

Bessant and Tidd (2007) suggest that social entrepreneurs exhibit many of the characteristics of other types of entrepreneurs. In other words they are:

1 *Ambitious*: they tackle major social issues, such as poverty, education, health, inequality, freedom of speech and justice. They are often driven by a desire or passion to make a difference, and have a high need for achievement.
2 *Mission-driven*: as discussed earlier, social entrepreneurs are more interested in creating social value than economic wealth; they are focused, hard working, energetic and driven in pursuit of their social vision.
3 *Strategic*: social entrepreneurs seek and act on opportunities; they see opportunities and make connections that others might miss. In addition, they create visions, make plans, rally resources and take action to make their vision a reality.
4 *Resourceful*: social entrepreneurs often start out as 'resource

less'; they often do not have ready access to the resources of an organization. They need to be exceptionally resourceful and skilled in networking, persuasion and building trust and credibility in order to mobilize human, financial and political resources.

5 *Results-orientated*: social entrepreneurs strive relentlessly towards the achievement of their vision.

The context for social entrepreneurship often carries its own specific challenges. As social entrepreneurship can take place in a number of different organizational contexts, the impact of different factors varies. Typically, however, the specific challenges facing social entrepreneurs are:

1 *Search for opportunities*: the social entrepreneur needs to search for new solutions to solve existing problems; most social problems are long standing, and many solutions have already been tried. The social entrepreneur needs a special ability to 'think outside the box', redefine the problem, make new connections, see beyond the present context and identify fruitful opportunities.

2 *Strategic selection*: once the social entrepreneur has spotted a context for making a difference, and has one or more proposed innovations, being able to move forward – and the choice and nature of the innovation – is highly dependent on garnering support. As discussed earlier, in existing organizations there may be varying levels of commitment to a social mission. For a new venture, or in a non-profit organization, the entrepreneur will need to identify possible funders and backers. Often, the social entrepreneur will need to build coalitions of support, as securing support for social innovation is often a very distributed process, involving many individual and organizational stakeholders.

3 *Implementation*: networking continues to be a core competence and activity during the implementation phase. Networking is essential to resource and capacity building, managing

relationships with key stakeholders, and creating commitment to, and alignment with, the vision. A key element of this process will be a clear and effectively communicated plan for translating the vision into a reality that engages and empowers key stakeholders. Since many social innovations involve many stakeholders, and often include public sector organizations, great persistence in navigating bureaucracy is likely to be necessary.

4 *Organization*: social innovation is highly people dependent. Limited, and too often inadequate, resources characterize the situation. Accordingly, social innovations are often dependent on rallying support from many sources; this means that organizational structures need to be loose and organic, and need to involve coalitions and joint working. The social entrepreneur needs to be adept at mobilizing support and accessing diverse resources through 'rich networks'. They also need to be comfortable working in situations where influence, rather than formal authority or power, is pivotal to making things happen.

Reflect: Think of something that you would like to change that would add social value for a community with which you identify. Would you seek to move things forward within an existing organization or start by gathering an ad hoc group of people around you? Make a quick list of some of the challenges that you would expect to encounter.

3.6 Entrepreneurial competencies

While discussion of entrepreneurial characteristics, attributes, traits and behaviours (Section 3.3) is useful in offering a basic understanding of the nature of entrepreneurship, increasing emphasis is being placed on developing understanding of entrepreneurial competencies, those competencies (skills, capabilities, knowledge and attitudes) that can be learned and developed towards enhancing an individual's capacity to succeed as an entrepreneur and innovator.

3.6.1 What is an entrepreneurial competence?

Entrepreneurial competencies have been identified as a specific group of competencies relevant to the exercise of successful entrepreneurship. Studies of entrepreneurial competences have focused on competencies associated with the development of small and new businesses (e.g. Colombo and Grilli, 2005; Nuthall, 2006), but there is increasing interest in corporate entrepreneurship and intrapreneurship (e.g. Hayton and Kelley, 2006; Sathe, 2003; Zahra, Nielsen and Bogner, 1999). Entrepreneurial competencies are seen as important to organizational survival, growth and success (Bird, 1995; Baum, 1994) and an understanding of the nature and role of such competencies can have important consequences for practice.

One of the challenges associated with understanding entre-preneurial competencies is the different ways in which the terms 'competency' and 'competence' are used. The terms competency and competence have been much discussed in the managerial literature, which embraces two distinct, but interrelated, meanings or uses of the term competency:

- *competency* as behaviours that an individual demonstrates
- *competencies* as minimum standards of performance (Strebler, Robinson and Heron, 1997).

In the US in the 1970s the idea of competencies was developed as part of an initiative by the American Management Association (AMA) to identify the characteristics which distinguish superior from average management performance (as discussed in Iles, 1993). Competencies are not seen as the task of the job, but rather that which enables people to do the task. These can be described in terms of essential personal traits, skills, knowledge and motives of the employee that lead to superior managerial performance (Boyatzis, 1982). This work focused on the concept of competency as an underlying characteristic of a person, which results in effective action and/or superior performance in a job.

In the UK, the focus has been on competence, which is a

description of something which a person who worked in a given occupational area should be able to do, or a description of an action, behaviour or outcome which a person should be able to demonstrate. The core agenda, worked out through government-sponsored bodies such as the Management Charter Initiative (MCI) and the National Council for Vocational Qualification (NCVQ), has been on securing standards for occupational competence and ensuring that vocational qualifications are based on this. The MCI management competence standards were published in 1990 as a form of competence framework, and the notion of a competence framework has been used for many different professional and vocational groups.

In summary, the two different terms, competency and competence, are linked but are distinct. Competence refers to the evaluation of performance in a specific domain of activity, whereas competency is a class of things that can be used to characterize individuals and their behaviours. Competencies are distinct from knowledge, skills and abilities in that they are not only attributes of individuals, but also depend on situation and social definition.

The distinction between competence and competency is equally applicable when considering entrepreneurial competencies (which contribute to success) and competence (as a minimum or baseline standard). Bird (1995) suggests that entrepreneurial competencies are defined as underlying characteristics such as specific knowledge, motives, traits, self-images, social roles and skills which result in venture birth, survival and/or growth. Man, Lau and Chan (2002) defined entrepreneurial competencies as the total ability of the entrepreneur to perform a job role successfully. Entrepreneurial competencies are exhibited by individuals who begin and/or transform their businesses. Some suggest that entrepreneurial competencies are needed to start a business, while managerial skills are needed to grow the business, although competence in entrepreneurship requires competencies in both areas (Man, Lau and Chan, 2002).

3.6.2 Frameworks of entrepreneurial competencies

There is considerable interest in establishing frameworks or lists of key entrepreneurial competencies. Typically such frameworks identify a number of key characteristics or skills and cluster these into competencies groups. Such an approach offers a more systematic approach to the description of complex sets of desired individual characteristics. An important and recurrent feature of such frameworks is the divide between managerial and entrepreneurial competencies. For example, in a relatively early study in this area, Chandler and Jansen (1992) sought to identify entrepreneurial, managerial and technical functions as the three roles that business founders must competently enact in order to be successful. They suggested that effective performance in the entrepreneurial role requires the founder to have the ability to recognize business opportunities and the drive to see firms through to fruition. Effective execution of the managerial role requires conceptual, interpersonal and political competence. To be competent in the technical role founders must be able to use the tools or procedures required in their specialized field. Similarly, Lerner and Almor (2002) found that managerial skills (finance, human resource management, operations and strategic management) and entrepreneurial skills (innovation and marketing) are separate, but necessary sets of skills. Rae (2007) discusses entrepreneurial management capabilities, and divides these into entrepreneurial capabilities and management capabilities, as shown in Table 3.8.

Table 3.8 *Entrepreneurial management capabilities (Rae, 2007)*	
Entrepreneurial capabilities	**Management capabilities**
Personal organization.	Leading and managing people.
Investigating opportunity.	Managing organization and operations.
Applying innovation.	Managing finance and resources.
Strategic venture planning.	Responsible management – social, legal, environmental and ethical responsibility.
Market development.	

Over the last two decades there have been a number of investigations in different contexts that have sought to generate lists of entrepreneurial competencies, with varying levels of categorization. Figure 3.4 seeks to summarize this work by generating a list that integrates the work of researchers in this area. Individual competencies have been categorized under four main headings which have been labelled as entrepreneurial competencies; business and management competencies; human relations competencies; and conceptual and relationship competencies. From this analysis, it is evident that a significant number of authors agree that the following competences are important for an entrepreneur: management skills, including the ability to develop management systems and organization and co-ordination skills; idea generation; conceptual and analytical competencies, including the ability to co-ordinate activities; customer management skills; delegation and motivation skills; the ability to recognize and take advantage of opportunities, the ability to formulate strategies for taking advantage of opportunities; hiring skills; decision-making skills; leadership skills; and commitment.

Reflect: Which of the four groups of competencies in Figure 3.4 is most relevant in supporting your entrepreneurial activity?
In what ways might you benefit from some development opportunities related to this group of competencies?

Most of the studies on entrepreneurial competencies focus on the commercial entrepreneurship associated with the establishment and development of a new business. While some of the competencies in such frameworks are also relevant to entrepreneurship in other contexts, such as corporate entrepreneurship, public entrepreneurship and social entrepreneurship, it is reasonable to speculate that the rather different context might demand a changed set of competencies to 'get the job done' and be successful. One such framework is that generated by Hayton and Kelley (2006) and shown in Table 3.9 (on page 93). This identifies

Entrepreneurial competencies
- Identification and definition of a viable market niche.
- Development of products or services appropriate to the firm's chosen market niche/product innovation.
- Idea generation.
- Environmental scanning.
- Recognizing, envisioning and taking advantage of opportunities.
- Formulating strategies for taking advantage of opportunities.

Business and management competencies
- Development of the management system necessary for the long term functioning of the organization.
- Acquisition and development of resources required to operate the firm.
- Business operational skills.
- Previous involvement with start-ups.
- Managerial experience.
- Familiarity with industry.
- Financial and budgeting skills.
- Previous experience.
- Management style.
- Marketing skills.
- Technical skills.
- Industry skills.
- The ability to implement strategy (develop programmes, budgets, procedures, and evaluate performance).
- Familiarity with the market.
- Business plan preparation.
- Goal setting skills.
- Management skills.

Human relations competencies
- Development of the organizational culture that management feel is necessary to guide the firm.
- Delegation skills.
- Ability to motivate others as individuals and in groups.
- Hiring skills.
- Human relations skills.
- Leadership skills.

Conceptual and relationship competencies
- Conceptual competencies.
- Organizational skills.
- Interpersonal skills.
- The ability to manage customers.
- Mental ability to co-ordinate activities.
- Written communication skills.
- Oral communication skills.
- Decision-making skills.
- Analytical skills.
- Logical thinking skills.
- Deal-making skills.
- Commitment competencies.

Figure 3.4 *Entrepreneurial competencies (Mitchelmore and Rowley, 2010)*

four types of entrepreneurial competencies, those being innovating, brokering, championing and sponsoring; and maps, respectively, knowledge, skills, personality and passion against these competency clusters to nurture and sustain innovation. They argue that the competencies of individual employees, specific to the pursuit of corporate entrepreneurship, are fundamental to an organization's ability to nurture and sustain innovation and new venture creation. And, therefore, employees in organizations seeking to promote corporate entrepreneurship need specific individual competencies in order to integrate existing and new knowledge and recognize, evaluate and capture entrepreneurial opportunities. They suggest that the following four competencies, while residing in individuals, also support the organizational goal of recognizing, evaluating and capturing entrepreneurial opportunities:

- *Innovating*: opportunity recognition, through having creative insight about particular knowledge and information combinations and what they can mean for users.
- *Brokering*: involving accessing new sources of information and knowledge, transferring this knowledge and combining different sources.
- *Championing*: identifying with, and taking responsibility for, the success of a project, through inspiring and enthusing others with a vision of the potential of an innovation.
- *Sponsoring*: helping entrepreneurs gain access to the resources that they need for their endeavours, through ensuring legitimacy and support for a project, and providing advice and guidance.

In conclusion, then, the notion of entrepreneurial competencies is important because it encourages the development of an understanding of the range of areas in which aspiring entrepreneurs need to develop their knowledge, skills, personal perspectives and motivations. As with earlier work on the traits and characteristics of entrepreneurs, a number of lists of relevant

Table 3.9 *Entrepreneurial competencies for corporate entrepreneurship and their associated knowledge, skills and personality (from Hayton and Kelley, 2006)*

	Innovating	Brokering	Championing	Sponsoring
Knowledge				
Specialized core	X	X		
Multidisciplinary	X	X	X	X
Organizational		X	X	X
Skills				
Cognitive ability	X	X		
Creativity	X	X		
Analogic reasoning		X	X	
Influencing		X	X	
Transformational leadership			X	X
Emotional intelligence		X	X	
Networking		X		
Personality				
Conscientiousness	X	X		
Openness to experience	X	X		
Confidence		X	X	
Credibility		X	X	
Risk tolerance			X	X
Tenacity	X	X	X	X
Passion	X	X	X	X

competencies, and sets of competencies, have been developed, and may vary in their applicability in different contexts. Nevertheless, there is a general agreement that both entrepreneurial and managerial competencies are necessary to successful entrepreneurial achievement.

Summary and conclusions

There are no simple answers to the questions 'What is entrepreneurship?' and 'What is an entrepreneur?' One of the big challenges emerging from the early work on entrepreneurs and their characteristics, that many of the characteristics or traits exhibited by entrepreneurs are also evident in managers, leaders and innovators in a variety of different contexts, supports the movement towards a notion of entrepreneurship that extends beyond the economic entrepreneurship associated with the establishment and growth of new business ventures, to embrace corporate entrepreneurship, public sector entrepreneurship and social entrepreneurship. On the other hand, the consideration of entrepreneurship across a wide range of different contexts presents its own definitional challenges. While acknowledging such ongoing debates concerning the essence of entrepreneurship, this chapter has endeavoured to distil some key perspectives in order to support entrepreneurs in developing their aspirations to make a difference into sustained, productive and effective entrepreneurial behaviour. The journey has included visits to the early trait and behavioural notions of entrepreneurship, and consideration of the special nature of public entrepreneurship and social entrepreneurship, and concluded with a tour of entrepreneurial competencies.

Review questions

1 Briefly discuss the development of the concept of 'entrepreneurship'.
2 What do you understand by the term 'entrepreneurial behaviour'? How does this differ from 'entrepreneurial characteristics'?
3 Corporate entrepreneurship is a term that can be used to refer to both individual behaviours and organizational behaviours. Explain the difference and the relationship between these two uses.
4 What are the key dimensions of corporate entrepreneurship?
5 Discuss the difference between a private entrepreneur and a public sector entrepreneur.
6 What, according to Pinchot, are the intrapreneur's ten commandments?
7 Discuss the potential barriers to innovation in the public sector.
8 Explain why it is difficult to define social entrepreneurship. Discuss possible ways towards resolving this difficulty.

9 Identify five characteristics that you associate with social entrepreneurs. What are the particular challenges that social entrepreneurs are likely to encounter?

10 Explain the two different but complementary meanings of 'competence'.

11 What is an entrepreneurial competency? Discuss one framework of entrepreneurial competencies.

Challenges

1 What does it mean to be an 'entrepreneur'?

2 Is it possible or desirable to expect every member of a team to be entrepreneurial?

3 Is it possible to be an entrepreneur in an organization that does not have an entrepreneurial culture?

4 Should a successful public sector corporate entrepreneur be expected to have the potential to make a success of founding and running their own business?

5 Can public sector organizations accommodate intrapreneurs while still being responsible and accountable?

6 How could the concept of 'social entrepreneurship' be more clearly delimited?

7 Is it reasonable to seek a universal set of entrepreneurial competencies that will apply in a range of different contexts?

Group discussion topics
Group discussion topic 1: Public sector corporate entrepreneurship

1 What benefits might/does your organization accrue from a more entrepreneurial approach?

2 What does your organization do to encourage staff to spot opportunities and convert them into innovations?

Group discussion topic 2: Social entrepreneurship

1 In relation to an innovation that you have been involved in and that has 'made a difference' for the people involved:
  • What made you get involved?
  • Where did the idea come from?
  • What challenges did you face in making the idea a reality?
  • How important was networking to the success of the project? How did you go about strengthening your networks to support the success of the project?
  • What plans have you for more innovations?

Group discussion topic 3: Entrepreneurial competencies

1 What characteristics or abilities do you have that do or could contribute to your success as an entrepreneur?
2 In what ways have these changed over the last few years?
3 What triggered these changes?
4 Can formal training or development activities help to develop entrepreneurial competencies?

References and additional reading

Antoncic, B. and Hisrich, R. D. (2001) Intrapreneurship: construct refinement and cross-cultural validation, *Journal of Business Venturing*, **16** (5), 495–527.

Antoncic, B. and Hisrich, R. D. (2003) Clarifying the Intrapreneurship Concept, *Journal of Small Business and Enterprise Development*, **10** (1), 7–24.

Austin, J., Stevenson, H. and Wei-Skillern, J. (2006) Social and Commercial Entrepreneurship: same, different, or both?, *Entrepreneurship Theory & Practice*, **30** (1), 1–22.

Barringer, B. R. and Ireland, R. D. (2008) *Entrepreneurship: successfully launching new ventures*, 2nd edn, Pearson Education International.

Baum, J. R. (1994) *The Relationship of Traits, Competencies,*

Motivation, Strategy and Structure to Venture Growth, PhD dissertation, University of Maryland, MD, USA.

Bessant, J. and Tidd, J. (2007) *Innovation and Entrepreneurship*, Wiley.

Binks, M. and Vale, P. (1990) *Entrepreneurship and Economic Change*, McGraw-Hill.

Bird, B. (1995) Towards a Theory of Entrepreneurial Competency. In Katz, J. (ed.), *Advances in Entrepreneurship, Firm Emergence and Growth*, Vol. 2, JAI Press, 51–72.

Borins, S. (2001) *The Challenge of Innovating in Government*, The PricewaterhouseCoopers Endowment for the Business of Government, February 2001.

Borins, S. (2002a) Leadership and Innovation in the Public Sector, *Leadership and Organization Development Journal*, **23** (8), 467–76.

Borins, S. (2002b) The Challenge of Innovating in Government. In Abramson, M. A. and Littman, I. D. (eds), *Innovation*, Rowman and Littlefield with PricewaterhouseCoopers Endowment for the Business of Government.

Boyatzis, R. E. (1982) *The Competent Manager: a model for effective performance*, Wiley.

Cantillon, R. (1755) *Essai Sur la Nature de Commerce en Général*, edited with an English translation by Henry Higgs, 1931, Macmillan for the Royal Economic Society.

Chandler, G. N. and Jansen, E. (1992) The Founder's Self-assessed Competence and Venture Performance, *Journal of Business Venturing*, **7** (3), 223–36.

Churchill, N. C. and Lewis, V. L. (1983) The Five Stages of Small Business Growth, *Harvard Business Review*, **61** (3), 1–12.

Colombo, M. G. and Grilli, L. (2005) Founders' Human Capital and the Growth of New Technology-based Firms: a competence-based view, *Research Policy*, **34** (6), 795–816.

Covin, J. G. and Miles, M. P. (1999) Corporate Entrepreneurship and the Pursuit of Competitive Advantage, *Entrepreneurship Theory and Practice*, **23** (3), 47–63.

Covin, J. G. and Slevin, D. P. (1989) Strategic Management of Small Firms in Hostile and Benign Environments, *Strategic Management Journal*, **10** (1), 75–88.

Damanpour, F. and Evan, W. M. (1984) Organizational Innovation and Performance: the problem of 'organizational lag', *Administrative Science Quarterly*, **29** (3), 392–409.

Gawthrop, L. (1999) Public Entrepreneurship in the Lands of Oz and Uz, *Public Integrity*, **1** (1), 75–86.

Gibb, A. A. (1993) Enterprising Culture: its meaning and implications for education and training, *Journal of European Industrial Training*, **11** (2), 2–38.

Hayton, J. C. and Kelley, D. J. (2006) A Competency-based Framework for Promoting Corporate Entrepreneurship, *Human Resource Management*, **45** (3), 407–27.

Heinonen, J. and Toivonen, J. (2008) Corporate Entrepreneurs or Silent Followers?, *Leadership & Organization Development Journal*, **29** (7), 583–99.

Herbert, R. and Link, A. (1982) *The Entrepreneur: mainstream views and radical critiques*, Praeger Publishers.

Iles, P. (1993) Achieving Strategic Coherence in HRD through Competence-based Management and Organization Development, *Personnel Review*, **22** (6), 63–80.

Kaplan, J. M. and Warren, A. C. (2007) *Patterns of Entrepreneurship*, 2nd edn, Wiley.

Kearney, C. and Kirzner, I. (1976) *The Economic Point of View: an essay in the history of economic thought*, 2nd edn, Sheed and Ward.

Kearney, C., Hisrich, R. and Roche, F. (2008) A Conceptual Model of Public Sector Corporate Entrepreneurship, *International Entrepreneurship and Management Journal*, **4** (3), 295-313.

Kirzner, I. M. (1973) *Competition and Entrepreneurship*, University of Chicago Press.

Knight, F. (1961) *Risk Uncertainty and Profit*, 2nd edn, Kelley.

Leibenstein, H. (1968) Entrepreneurship and Development, *American Economic Review*, **58** (2), 72–83.

Lerner, M. and Almor, T. (2002) Relationships among Strategic
  Capabilities and the Performance of Women-owned Small
  Ventures, *Journal of Small Business Management*, **40** (2), 109–25.
Luchsinger, V. and Bagby, D. R. (1987) Entrepreneurship and
  Intrapreneurship Behaviors, Comparisons, and Contrasts, *SAM
  Advanced Management Journal*, **52**, 10–13.
Man, T., Lau, T. and Chan, K. F. (2002) The Competitiveness of
  Small and Medium Enterprises: a conceptualisation with focus
  on entrepreneurial competencies, *Journal of Business
  Venturing*, **17** (2), 123–42.
McClelland, D. (1961) *The Achieving Society*, Van Nostrand.
McGrath, R. and MacMillan, I. (2000) *The Entrepreneurial
  Mindset*, Harvard Business School Press.
Miller, D. (1983) The Correlates of Entrepreneurship in Three
  Types of Firms, *Management Science*, **29** (7), 770–91.
Mitchelmore, S. and Rowley, J. (2010) Entrepreneurial
  Competencies: a literature review and development agenda,
  *International Journal of Entrepreneurial Behaviour and
  Research*, **16** (2), 92–111.
Neck, H., Brush, C. and Allen, E. (2009) The Landscape of Social
  Entrepreneurship, *Business Horizons*, **52** (1), 13–19.
Nuthall, P. L. (2006) Determining the Important Management
  Skill Competences: the case of family farm business in New
  Zealand, *Agricultural Systems*, **88** (2/3), 429–50.
Peredo, A. M. and McLean, M. (2006) Social Entrepreneurship: a
  critical review of the concept, *Journal of World Business*, **41** (1),
  56–65.
Pinchot, G. III (1985) *Intrapreneuring: why you don't have to leave
  the corporation to become an entrepreneur*, Harper & Row.
Rae, D. (2007) *Entrepreneurship: from opportunity to action*,
  Palgrave Macmillan.
Rainey, H., Backoff, R. and Levin, C. H. (1976) Comparing Public
  and Private Organizations, *Public Administration Review*, **36**
  (2), 233–44.
Sadler, R. J. (2000) Corporate Entrepreneurship in the Public

Sector: the dance of the chameleon, *Australian Journal of Public Administration,* **59** (2), 25–43.

Sathe, V. (2003) *Corporate Entrepreneurship: top managers and new business creation,* Cambridge University Press.

Schumpeter, J. (1934) *The Theory of Economic Development: an inquiry into profits, capital, credit, interest and the business cycle,* Harvard University Press.

Strebler, M., Robinson, D. and Heron, P. (1997) *Getting the Best out of your Competencies,* Institute of Employment Studies.

Wilson, J. (1989) *Bureaucracy: what government agencies do and why they do it,* Basic Books.

Zahra, S. A. (1991) Predictors and Financial Outcomes of Corporate Entrepreneurship: an exploratory study, *Journal of Business Venturing,* **6** (4), 259–85.

Zahra, S. Z., Nielsen, A. P. and Bogner, W. C. (1999) Corporate Entrepreneurship, Knowledge, and Competence Development, *Entrepreneurship Theory and Practice,* **23** (1), 169–89.

Zerbinati, S. and Souitaris, V. (2005) Entrepreneurship in the Public Sector: a framework of analysis in European local governments, *Entrepreneurship & Regional Development,* **17** (1), 43–64.

4

Organizing for innovation

Learning objectives

After reading this chapter you should be able to:

- Discuss what is meant by innovativeness and an innovative organization.
- Evaluate different perspectives on how innovation can be supported in organizations.
- Reflect on the processes associated with cultivating a creative and innovative organizational climate.
- Understand the role and nature of leadership in organizational innovation.
- Reflect on the characteristics of creative and innovative teams.
- Discuss the importance of an innovation strategy.
- Be sensitive to the challenges associated with launching into an internal market, and associated change management processes.

4.1 Introduction

This chapter draws together and develops further a number of themes that have been visited in earlier chapters in this book. Most importantly, this chapter returns to the topics of innovation management and innovation orientation and cultures which were introduced at the end of Chapter 2 and continues consideration of the organizational context for innovation. It also takes into account the nature and challenges of public sector entrepreneurship as explored in Chapter 3. Other sections focus specifically on innovation leadership, innovation teams, innovation strategy and the change management associated with innovation implementation.

Throughout this chapter are intermingled considerations of entrepreneurship, innovation, and creativity, entrepreneurial orientation, innovation orientation and creative organizations. This approach is adopted counter to authors who see innovation and entrepreneurship as separate processes, in the belief that there is actually a considerable overlap. As Ireland, Kuratko and Morris suggest:

> Corporate entrepreneurship is a process used in established firms seeking to use innovation as the means to pursue entrepreneurial opportunities. Corporate entrepreneurship helps a firm to create new businesses through product and process innovation and market developments and fosters the strategic renewal of existing operations.
>
> (Ireland, Kuratko and Morris, 2006, 12)

We add creativity into the mix because it is widely recognized to be tightly coupled with innovation (as discussed in Chapter 1), and, specifically, considerations of discussions of creative organizational climates complement those discussions associated with the characteristics of innovative organizations.

4.2 Innovativeness, innovation orientation and entrepreneurial orientation

Organizations have different levels of innovativeness. According to Lumpkin and Dess:

> Innovativeness reflects a firm's tendency to engage in and support new ideas, novelty, experimentation, and creative processes that may result in new products, services, or technological processes . . . innovativeness represents a basic willingness to depart from existing technologies or practices and venture beyond the current state of the art.
>
> (Lumpkin and Dess, 1996, 142)

Reflect: *The following are some ways in which evidence can be gathered to assess the level of an organization's innovativeness:*

- *Ask managers about their willingness to discard old beliefs and explore new alternatives, and the way in which they value and reward experimentation.*
- *Measure the 'entrepreneurial mindset' or 'creative capacity' of a sample of staff.*
- *Identify the level of resource dedicated to research and development.*
- *Identify the proportion of professionals and specialists in an organization.*
- *Count the number of new product or service introductions and the frequency of changes in services or product lines.*

(developed from Lumpkin and Dess, 1996)

Which of these would be most appropriate for measuring the level of innovativeness in your organization?

'Entrepreneurial intensity' (EI) is a similar concept to 'innovativeness' when applied to an organization. It was introduced by Ireland, Kuratko and Morris (2006) as a measure of the level of entrepreneurship in an organization. They suggest that EI has two dimensions:

1 *Frequency of entrepreneurship*: how many entrepreneurial initiatives is the company pursuing?
2 *Degree of entrepreneurship*: to what extent do those initiatives represent incremental or modest steps versus bold breakthroughs?

Measuring both of these dimensions will give an audit of an organization's level of entrepreneurial activity, and provide a basis for benchmarking over time, and with similar organizations.

High levels of innovativeness, or entrepreneurial intensity, within an organization do not just happen; they need to be cultivated and supported. Innovative organizations do not just wait for innovation to happen; they have culture and structures that encourage innovation, creativity and entrepreneurship, and processes and systems to convert ideas into marketable products and services. Siguaw, Simpson and Enz (2006) describe such organizations as innovation oriented (see Chapter 2).

Closely related to the concept of innovation orientation is the concept of entrepreneurial orientation (EO). Entrepreneurial orientation refers to the strategy-making processes and styles of firms that engage in entrepreneurial activities. As we have seen earlier, such activities typically involve innovation, and indeed in the widely acknowledged model of EO proposed by Lumpkin and Dess one of the dimensions of EO is proposed to be innovativeness. Lumpkin and Dess (1996) suggest that EO has five dimensions:

1 *Autonomy*: key organizational players are enabled to take action free of stifling organizational constraints.
2 *Innovativeness*: the firm's tendency to engage in and support new ideas, novelty, experimentation and creative processes that may result in new products, services or technological processes.
3 *Risk taking*: proclivity to engage in risky projects and managers' preference for bold versus cautious acts to achieve organizational objectives.
4 *Proactiveness*: acting in anticipation of future problems, needs or changes, and seizing the initiative in the marketplace.
5 *Competitive aggressiveness*: propensity to directly and intensely challenge its competitors to achieve entry or to improve position, and to outperform rivals in the marketplace.

While arguing that these are the five dimensions or behaviours of entrepreneurial orientation, Lumpkin and Dess (2001) suggest that these dimensions vary in their importance depending on context. Specifically, they suggest that proactiveness, or response to opportunities, is an appropriate mode for firms in dynamic environments or in growth stage industries where conditions are rapidly changing and opportunities are numerous. But, competitive aggressiveness, a response to threats, is more appropriate in hostile environments and in mature industries where competition for customers and resources is intense. Most importantly, these findings suggest that there is unlikely to be one model for either innovation orientation or entrepreneurial orientation that suits all organizations, and indeed even an individual organization may need to change its emphasis on specific dimensions or aspects of its innovative behaviour over time. In other words, each organization needs to develop its own entrepreneurship and innovation strategy, informed by sound research and theoretical frameworks, and benchmarked against best practice elsewhere.

Reflect: Is your information organization in a dynamic and rapidly changing market environment where there are lots of opportunities? Or in a mature market environment where competition for customers and resources is intense?

4.3 The innovative organization
This section presents a range of different perspectives, from key thinkers, on the components and characteristics of an innovative, entrepreneurial and creative organization. The reader is invited to choose one, or to seek to integrate two or more perspectives, and to use these models and ideas as a basis for reflecting on innovation in their information organization.

4.3.1 Components and characteristics of an innovative organization
Innovative and entrepreneurial organizations need to operate in such a way that they enable and facilitate their staff to deploy their creativity and work together to create innovations and change that

are in the interests of the organization. Further, they need to do this in a way that is appropriate for the organization and its stakeholders. Different organizations may be in different 'market' environments, need to prioritize different types of innovation, and need to engage to different extents in radical and incremental innovation. Successful innovation is dependent upon making an effective link between both the innovation process and its outcomes that is appropriate for the organization at a specific point in time. Innovative organizations not only know how to innovate, they also know how to manage their innovation climate and processes and to adapt them as necessary. Bessant and Tidd (2007) suggest that the innovative organization has the components listed in Table 4.1.

Reflect: Consider the components of an innovative organization as listed in Table 4.1. Rate your organization on each of these components on a score of 1 to 5 (1=low; 5=high). What does this tell you about your organization? Is this profile appropriate for the context in which the organization finds itself?

On the basis of a study of non-profit and governmental organizations, Light (1998) suggested that those organizations that were able to consistently innovate had:

1 a commitment to controlling their environments rather than the other way round
2 an internal structure that creates the freedom to imagine
3 leadership that prepares the organization to innovate
4 management systems that serve the mission of the organization rather than the other way round.

Ireland, Kuratko and Morris (2006) approach supporting innovation and entrepreneurship from the perspective of corporate entrepreneurship. They suggest that the key characteristics of a work environment that supports corporate entrepreneurship are structure, controls, culture and human resource management, as

Table 4.1 *Components of the innovative organization (Bessant and Tidd, 2007)*

Component	Key features
Shared vision, leadership and the will to innovate	Clearly articulated and shared sense of purpose. Stretching strategic intent. 'Top management commitment'
Appropriate structure	Organization design which enables creativity, learning and interaction. An appropriate balance between organic and mechanistic options to suit the context.
Key individuals	Promoters, champions, gatekeepers and other roles which energize or facilitate innovation.
Effective team working	Appropriate use of teams (at local, cross-functional and interorganizational level). Investment in team selection and building.
Continuing and stretching individual development	Long-term commitment to education and training to ensure high levels of competence and effective learning skills.
Open communication	Internally – upwards, downward and laterally. Between the organizations and external partners and stakeholders.
High involvement in innovation	Participation in organization-wide continuous improvement activity encompassing a number of different types of innovation, to generate relevant change, and innovation experience.
External focus	Internal and external customer orientation. Extensive networking. Gathering competitive intelligence to understand the 'market environment'.
Creative climate	Positive approach to creative ideas,, supported by relevant motivation systems.
Organizational learning	Commitment to learning and development, including learning how to learn and how to innovate.

shown in Figure 4.1. In relation to structure, they argue specifically for organic structure with relatively few layers, broad spans of control and a high level of decentralization of authority and responsibility. They argue that these structural characteristics facilitate the surfacing of ideas, and innovations throughout the organization. On the other hand, they agree with Bessant and Tidd (2007) that key consideration needs to be lent to an appropriate level of control to strike a balance between encouraging individual action through flexibility, and ensuring co-ordination, consistency and accountability through tight control. They also recognize the importance of a culture that empowers people to act creatively. Finally, they emphasize the role of Human Resource Management Systems (HRMS) which have considerable scope to influence behaviour through recruitment, selection, promotion and careers, training and developing, and rewards. All of these activities present opportunities to promote and develop entrepreneurial behaviour.

Structure	Controls
Horizontal over vertical.	Control based on 'no surprises'.
Few layers.	Loose–tight control properties.
Broader spans of control.	Resource slack.
Decentralization.	Internal venture capital pools.
Cross-functional processes.	Emphasis on self-control.
Less formalization.	Empowerment and discretion.
Open communication flow.	Mutual trust.
Sense of smallness.	Open information sharing.
Human resource management	**Culture**
Jobs that are broad in scope.	Entrepreneurial learning.
Multiple career paths.	Balanced individual–collective emphasis.
Extensive job socialization.	Emphasis on excellence.
Individual and group rewards.	Emotional commitment.
High employee involvement in	Freedom to grow and fail.
appraisals.	Emphasis on results over process.
Longer-term reward emphasis.	Celebration of innovation.
Appraisal and reward criteria include	Healthy dissatisfaction and a sense of
innovativeness and risk taking.	urgency.
	Focus on the future.

Figure 4.1 *Characteristics of a work environment that supports corporate entrepreneurship (Ireland, Kuratko and Morris, 2006)*

4.3.2 Innovative climate and culture

As is evident from the lists in Table 4.1 and Figure 4.1, organizational culture has an important role in encouraging or blocking innovation. Organizational culture has a significant impact on the experience of working in an organization, how the organization is perceived by customers and other stakeholders, and on organizational performance. Culture is a somewhat slippery and elusive concept, but all innovators need to understand organizational culture and the way in which the organization works. Further, managers seeking to develop an innovative organization need to engage with and seek to evolve organizational cultures in order to enhance the organization's innovativeness. In addition, the success of many process and service innovations is often highly dependent on organizational culture, and such innovations may challenge existing cultures. Indeed, the change process associated with, say, a process innovation that involved the restructuring and redefinition of job roles would typically change people's role, the skills required of them, and the other members of staff with whom they interact. This challenges their 'comfort zones' (notions of who they are and what they do) and 'cliques' (the people with whom they identify, gossip and exchange mutual support). Thus, such an innovation is a golden opportunity to encourage people to think and behave differently.

So innovation and organizational culture are tightly coupled, but what is organizational culture? Huczynski and Buchanan define organizational culture thus:

> The collection of relatively uniform and enduring values, beliefs and customs, traditions and practices that are shared by an organization's members, learned by new recruits and transmitted from one generation of employees to the next.
>
> (Huczynski and Buchanan, 2007, 623)

Schein's (1985) model of organizational culture elaborates further. This model proposes that there are three levels of culture: surface manifestation, values, and basic assumptions, and that these three levels interact. Importantly, this model differentiates between surface manifestations and basic assumptions. Surface manifestations (such as artefacts, ceremonials, courses, heroes, language and behavioural norms) may be managed and manipulated by managers and leaders. On the other hand, basic assumptions regarding, for example, the nature of reality, truth, human activity and relationships, are much more difficult to change. Mediating between surface manifestation and basic assumptions are organizational values, or the things that are important to the organization. Values are often unspoken, but are deeply embedded in the basic assumptions of the organization.

Creating an innovative culture where one does not already exist is likely to be a challenging and slow process, but may be facilitated by dispersed innovation centred on a network of innovation promoters and gatekeepers spread throughout the organization. As discussed in Chapter 3, public sector innovators often work in an environment in which there are strong basic assumptions about the nature of public service, how it should be delivered and the employment status of staff. Individual innovators are unlikely to be able to change these assumptions, but the most successful corporate entrepreneurs will work to understand the culture sufficiently to be able to navigate within it.

The rather more ideal scenario for a corporate entrepreneur is an organization that has an innovative culture or climate. The presence of such a culture is also likely to enhance the innovation performance of the organization.

A recent survey by the Chartered Management Institute (Patterson and Kerrin, 2009) focused on the role of innovation in recovery. They use the dimensions in Table 4.2 as a basis for profiling the extent to which organizations currently encourage innovations and how far they seek to build an innovative culture. Responses are based on managers' views, but do demonstrate that most managers provide support for new ideas and their application. As indicated in Table 4.2 most managers appreciate the importance

Table 4.2 *Factors that drive innovation in organizations (Patterson and Kerrin, 2009)*

Factor	% agreement
Managers provide practical support for new ideas and their application.	69
There is a 'we are in it together' attitude.	69
We strive for a reputation for being innovative.	67
The general management style is participative and collaborative.	66
The organizational goals are directly aligned with innovation.	54
Management practices actively enhance innovation.	53
There is a 'no blame' culture – mistakes are talked about freely so that other people can learn from them.	51
Resources and facilities are readily available for use in testing out new ideas.	47
Personal development objectives explicitly related to innovation are set.	34
Job assignments ensure that there is enough time and scope for trying out new ideas.	34
The appraisal system is directly linked to rewarding creativity and innovation.	32
Innovative thinking is often stifled.	17

of support from management for new ideas, there is a 'we're in it together' culture, and organizations are striving to acquire a reputation for innovation. However, lower down the table in Table 4.2 there are areas for concern, and also, it is important to remember, if 69% of managers think that their organizations support new ideas, for example, that leaves 31% who do not feel that such support is available. Indeed Table 4.3 shows that there is a difference between public and private sectors by summarizing the statements on which differences between sectors are apparent.

Reflect: *Compare Table 4.1, Figure 4.1 and Table 4.2. What are the factors that they all agree are important in promoting innovation in organizations?*

Table 4.3 *Working practice cited as more prevalent in the private sector than the public sector (Patterson and Kerrin, 2009)*

	Private sector organizations % agreement	Public sector organizations % agreement
We strive for a reputation for being innovative.	74	63
The general management style is participative and collaborative.	73	60
There is a 'no blame' culture – mistakes are talked about freely so that other people can learn from them.	60	44
Resources and facilities are readily available for use in testing out new ideas.	54	36
Job assignments ensure that there is enough time and scope for trying out new ideas.	40	29
The appraisal system is directly linked to rewarding creativity and innovation.	34	29

4.3.3 Creative organizations

The concept of the creative organization has many similarities with that of the innovative or entrepreneurial organization. Further, library and information commentators and researchers have been particularly interested in creativity (Coveney, 2008; Heye, 2006; Walton, 2008). For these two reasons our discussion of organizational cultures and climates is continued, in order to visit briefly the notions of the creative organization and creative teams.

Innovation and creativity are often closely coupled. Many authors, including many in the library and information field, view the distinction between creativity and innovation as being associated with the initial stages in the innovation process. They suggest that creativity is the generation of ideas and that innovation is the implementation of those ideas (Amabile et al., 1996; Ensor, Cottam and Band, 2001; Harvard Business School, 2003; Coveney, 2008). This is not the position that this author takes, believing that there is just as much creativity required in the implementation stages of the innovation process as there is in the earlier stages of idea generation and opportunity recognition. However, there is no disputing that creative work by both individuals and teams is an essential ingredient of innovation. As Amabile et al. say:

> Creativity is the seed of all innovation, and psychological perceptions of innovation (the implementation of people's ideas) within an organization are likely to impact the motivation to generate new ideas.

> (Amabile et al., 1996, 1155)

One of the most widely used (and criticized!) models of the work environment dimensions that impact on creativity is the KEYS model for assessing the climate for creativity developed by Amabile et al. (1996), the key scales in which are shown in Table 4.4 (after Coveney, 2008). An important contribution of Amabile et al.'s (1996) work is that it considers both aspects of the environment that might support creativity (stimulant scales), as well as those that might impede creativity (obstacle scales). Coveney (2008) has used the KEYS scales to investigate creativity in a UK public library service. She concludes that library managers need to take responsibility for establishing the right work environment alongside adopting an innovation strategy for the implementation of new ideas.

Other commentators on creativity in libraries are ambivalent about the ability of library professionals to be creative and that of library managers to develop creative organizations. Walton (2008) reports on a number of initiatives for promoting creativity and innovation in libraries, but other commentators are less positive. Hourston (2006, 35), for example, suggests that there is a stereotype that librarians are 'just about as uncreative as anybody can be'. Schacter (2005) suggests that the challenge is to simultaneously engage in creativity and continue to do what librarians are good at – creating order from chaos. In the absence of definitive evidence the opportunity is to challenge the stereotype.

Reflect: Compare the stimulant scales in Table 4.4 with Table 4.1. What are the similarities and differences? Can you think of any reason for these?

Table 4.4 *The KEYS work environment for creativity scales (Amabile et al., 1996; Coveney, 2008)*

Scale name	Description
Stimulant scales	
Organizational encouragement	An organizational culture that encourages creativity through the firm constructive judgement of ideas, reward and recognition for creative work, mechanisms for developing new ideas, an active flow of ideas, and a shared vision of what the organization is trying to do.
Supervisory encouragement	A supervisor who serves as a good work model, sets goals appropriately, supports the work groups, values individual contributions, and shows confidence in the work group.
Work group supports	A diversely skilled work group in which people communicate well, are open to new ideas, constructively challenge each other's work, trust and help each other and feel committed to the work they are doing.
Freedom	Freedom in deciding what work to do or how to do it; a sense of control over one's work.
Sufficient resources	Access to appropriate resources, including funds, materials, facilities and information.
Challenging work	A sense of having to work hard on challenging tasks and important projects.
Obstacle scales	
Organizational impediments	An organizational culture that impedes creativity through political problems. Harsh criticism of new ideas, destructive internal competition, an avoidance of risk, and an overemphasis on the status quo.
Workload pressure	Extreme time pressures, unrealistic expectations for productivity, distractions from creative work.

4.3.4 Barriers to innovation and creativity

So far we have discussed the factors that support innovation in organizations. For the persistent innovator or entrepreneur, support may be less important than stifling constraints. Table 4.5 lists some of the factors that have been cited as having the potential to stifle innovation. If you are aware that most of these factors are exhibited in your organization that might well explain the difficulties associated with innovation and change.

Reflect: Compare the two columns in Table 4.5. To what extent can these two lists be mapped onto one another?

Table 4.5 *Constraints on innovation in organizations*

Factors that stifle innovation (Kanter, 2003)	Constraints on innovation (Patterson and Kerrin, 2009) (ranked in order of significance)
Dominance of restrictive vertical relationships.	Excessive financial constraints.
Poor lateral communications.	Lack of time.
Limited tools and resources.	Lack of resources.
Top-down dictates.	Risk aversion and a fear of failure among leaders.
Formal, restricted vehicles for change.	Too hierarchical a structure across staff levels.
Reinforcement of a culture of inferiority ('good innovations come from outside').	Unclear leadership strategy and goals towards innovation.
Unfocused innovative activity	Insufficient incentives in place to encourage innovation.
Unsupportive accounting practices.	Insufficient training and development resources for innovative ideas.
	Insufficient talent for innovation.
	Lack of autonomy in job roles.
	Insufficient opportunities and mechanisms to share knowledge with others.
	A lack of support from managers.

4.3.5 Towards an innovative organization

In conclusion, here we have drawn together a number of the main perspectives on the factors that promote and support, or hinder, innovation, entrepreneurship and creativity in organizations. These perspectives have some overlapping themes, but there is no consensus. This is not surprising since innovation is a complex concept which is understood and enacted differently by different organizations and different professional groups. These perspectives are useful as a basis for reflection on the journey towards making your information organization more innovative. Each innovator, leader and manager needs to decide which is the best way forward for their organization. This includes striking the right balance between adaptability (the ability to plan for the future) and alignment (the ability to deal with the present) (Birkenshaw and Gibson, 2005).

In the next few sections we focus in more detail on some specific aspects of organizing for innovation.

4.4 Leadership for innovation

A recent CMI study (Patterson and Kerrin, 2009) asked respondents to identify the top three catalysts of innovation in their organization. Almost half of those asked identified managers' support and openness to innovation as being critical. Four in ten pointed to the role of leaders in modelling behaviours that encourage innovation, while almost a third highlighted the importance of setting up the right team of people. This is a strong endorsement of the importance of management and leadership in promoting and encouraging innovation. The pivotal role of leadership is emphasized by many of the commentators on creativity and innovation in the library and information field (e.g. Akeroyd, 2000; Walton, 2008).

Paul (2000) suggests that a library manager around whom creativity will flourish needs to be candid, highly communicative and open to participation by others in decision-making processes. An ability and willingness to co-operate extensively on an equal basis with other staff members is also important. They need to lead by example, by showing initiative and creativity in themselves. Walton (2008, 129) suggests that 'changing a library's culture is not easy, but organizations will benefit massively if creativity is accepted as a basic cultural norm'.

On this basis, the simplest way to summarize the role of leadership is to reflect and take action on the characteristics of an innovative and creative organization (as discussed earlier in this chapter) towards engendering a more innovative and creative culture and climate.

In order to consider the role of leaders in innovation further, it is useful to revisit the essence of leadership. Leaders are influencers; they influence others towards the achievement of goals. They are externally focused, have vision, are strategists and catalysts, and look to the future. Effective leaders are involved in:

- creating, sharing and communicating vision
- shaping culture
- developing the potential of others
- connecting with people and building successful relationships
- taking a holistic and wide perspective.

(Roberts and Rowley, 2008)

Importantly, information professionals who are not managers may meet these criteria and play a leadership role. They may contribute, for example, to developing others or to building strong networks and relationships. The notion that leadership can be carried out at all levels in an organization, and is not the exclusive domain of managers and senior staff, is termed 'dispersed leadership'. Indeed, leadership and innovation are often tightly coupled such that it is not unreasonable to propose that being an innovator is very much the same thing as being a leader.

Research by the Advanced Institute of Management Research with the Chartered Management Institute focusing on the role of leaders in innovation (AIMR, 2005) suggests that leaders have a dual role in innovation:

- *as motivators*: inspiring people to transcend the ordinary
- *as architects*: designing an organizational environment that enables employees to be innovative.

The research distinguishes between leaders who primarily motivate through transformational actions (motivators) and those who have a more transactional approach, which focuses on the co-ordination of organizational tasks (architects). Based on the SHL Universal Competency Framework, Table 4.6 shows the behavioural focus of these two different types of leadership, and their associated competences, in four key areas of leadership.

Table 4.6 *Comparing transactional and transformational leadership*

	Transactional focus	Transformational focus
Developing the vision: the strategy domain	• Analysing. • Learning and researching. • Entrepreneurial and commercial thinking.	• Creating and innovating. • Formulating strategies and concepts. • Adapting and responding to change.
Sharing the goals: the communication domain	• Presenting and communicating information. • Writing and reporting.	• Relating and networking. • Persuading and influencing.
Gaining support: the people domain	• Working with people. • Adhering to principles and values.	• Leading and supervising.
Delivering success: the operational domain	• Planning and organizing. • Delivering results. • Coping with pressure and setbacks.	• Deciding and initiating action.

Reflect: It might be argued that as motivators leaders need a transformational focus, whereas as architects they need a transactional focus. Thinking of yourself or someone you know well, are you/they primarily transactional or transformational leaders, and what does this imply for your/their approach to innovation leadership?

In the context of change leadership, which is closely associated with innovation leadership, Dunphy and Stace (1990) suggest four different contingent leadership styles on the basis of the scale of the change (Tables 4.7 and 4.8). They suggest that the optimum style depends on the scale of the change.

Opinions are divided as to the most appropriate way to characterize leaders, whether by their personal traits, their behaviours or styles, or by their competencies and abilities, but there is a general agreement that a key skill required of leaders is to be able to adapt their approach to context, and that the most appropriate leadership is contingent on context. This is especially true for innovation leadership, since different scales and types of innovation may demand different levels of emphasis on task and on people, and different approaches to establishing direction and

Table 4.7 *Dunphy and Stace's (1990) contingent change leadership styles*

	Incremental change strategies	Transformative change strategies
Collaborative-consultative modes	**Participative evolution** Suitable for minor adjustment where time is available and where key interest groups can be brought on board.	**Charismatic transformation** Suitable for major adjustment where there is little time for participation and where there is support for radical change.
Directive-coercive modes	**Forced evolution** Suitable for minor adjustment, where time is available, but key interest groups oppose change.	**Dictatorial transformation** Suitable for major adjustment where there is no time for participation and where there is no internal support for major change that is necessary for survival.

Table 4.8 *Change leaders for Dunphy and Stace's (1990) change leadership styles*

Type of change leadership style	Type of change leader	Description
Participative evolution	Coaches	People-centred, inspirational communicators.
Forced evolution	Captains	Systematic, task-oriented authority figures.
Charismatic transformation	Charismatics	Heroic figures who are able to sell their own dramatic and challenging vision to others and carry others with them.
Dictatorial transformation	Commanders	Purposeful, decisive, tough-minded, forceful, with an ability to neutralize or remove resistance.

strategy and managing their implementation. This makes leadership challenging but no less necessary. Mumford et al. (2002) regard creative work as being contextualized, in that creativity depends on the capabilities, pressures, resources and socio-technical system in which employees work. In order for creativity to flourish, leaders need to ensure that the structure of the work environment, the climate and culture, and the human resources practices (such as rewards, goals, resources and performance evaluations) are designed to facilitate creative outcomes. Shalley and Gilson (2004) suggest that this context needs to be considered at the individual, job, group or team, and organizational levels, and that leadership has an important role at all levels. On the basis of an extensive review of previous research they suggest that leaders who seek to promote creativity focus on:

1 *Developing a supportive work context*: this takes into account how leaders interact with employees; how co-workers, team members, and even those outside of work interact with employees; whether sufficient resources are available; how employees expect to be rewarded and evaluated; and whether the climate is perceived to be 'fair'. Such job-level factors should be prioritized because they have the most immediate and critical effect on employees' experience and, therefore, creativity.

2 *Communicating that creativity is valued*: leaders should communicate clearly that creativity is welcome. This may be achieved through, for example, setting goals and role requirements. In addition, it may involve leaders being creative themselves, or encouraging others who are creative to act as role models and to mentor others. Rewards are an important indicator of desired behaviours.

3 *Designing the team and social context for creativity*: leaders should ensure that individuals come in contact with people that have a diverse range of skills and interests; they need to encourage interaction across functional areas, and among team members and with employees outside of the team. Leaders also need to monitor and develop team climates and cultures that value and support creativity.

4 *Developing individuals' creativity*: this may start with seeking out and appointing individuals who are creative, placing creative individuals in contexts in which their creativity is an asset and not a hindrance, and offering training in problem solving and other skills that support creativity.

In addition to leaders there are other key roles or project champions that contribute to the success of innovation; leaders or others may variously adopt these roles. These include:

- *Technical champion or inventor*: the person who has the critical technical knowledge to understand a problem, to propose a solution, and to solve the developmental problems associated with bringing the innovation to fruition; this role requires inspiration, motivation and commitment.
- *Organizational sponsor*: the person who has the power and influence in the organization to smooth the progress of the innovation, including resource allocation, often from a top management position. The key requirement is that the sponsor believes in the potential of the innovation.
- *Project leader*: the project team leader, who can be granted the authority to 'make the innovation happen'.
- *Business innovator*: the person who focuses on the market or user perspective, and who ensures a fit between the innovation and market opportunity, as both evolve during the development process.
- *Technological gatekeeper*: the person who collects information from various sources (often informal) and passes it to key individuals; the gatekeeper's role is to facilitate communication within a team and between the team and other key individuals and groups. This role is particularly important in distributed or virtual teams.

Reflect: Which of the roles discussed in this section would you most enjoy? Can you think of a context in which you would be able to develop your experience of this role?

4.5 Building innovative and creative teams

Innovation and creativity in organizations are achieved to a large extent by team working. Indeed, important writers on organizations such as Handy (1993) and Belbin (1981) have promoted the idea that an organization is a collection of groups rather than a collection of individuals. Groups are seen as fundamental to organizational success, individual motivation and job satisfaction. Accordingly, there has been much focus on the creation and development of teams and 'team working'. Roberts and Rowley (2004) suggest that the types of teams shown in Table 4.9 are commonly used in library and information services. Any of these types could either be involved in an innovation, or, in the case of the cross-functional team, the self-managing team or a network, be constituted specifically to manage a specific innovation project.

Reflect: Choose two of the team types in Table 4.9. Which do you think would be best at (a) new service development, and (b) continuous improvement of service delivery?

According to Tidd, Bessant and Pavitt (2005), groups have more to offer than individuals in respect of fluency of idea generation, and in flexibility of solutions developed. Research suggests that high performance project teams rarely happen by accident. They are the result of careful selection, enhanced by investment in teambuilding, clear guidance on roles and tasks and attention to the social aspects of group processes as well as the task aspects. An assorted group of people does not become a team without considerable effort on the part of the team leader and members. Groups need to go through the group formation process proposed by Tuckman and Jensen (1997) of:

- *Forming*: the group starts the process of organizing itself to achieve common goals, but with a high level of uncertainty and anxiety. The role of the team leader is to establish goals and directions.
- *Storming*: the group experiments, gains confidence, listens, explores issues. Conflict and tensions are common, and the leader's role is to resolve these.
- *Norming*: the group consolidates, resolves problems, starts to

Table 4.9 *Types of groups and teams in library and information services (based on Roberts and Rowley, 2004)*

Type of group	Purpose
Operational	Distribution of work. Management and control. Processing information. Co-ordination and liaison.
Strategic	Problem solving. Decision making. Future direction. Co-ordination and liaison.
Cross-functional teams/matrix management	Problem solving in relation to a specific issue or theme. Co-ordination and liaison. Consultation and participation – drawing on a range of staff from different areas within the organization.
Multiskilled or hybrid teams	Similar to the cross-functional team, the emphasis is on drawing together staff with the right mix of needed skills, e.g. marketing, ICT, creativity. These teams can also draw on staff from outside the service.
Self-managing /self-directed teams	This type of team could apply to any of the team types above; it describes teams that work autonomously with little overt control from a manager. Such teams are seen to be more effective, with staff more motivated and involved.
Virtual teams	Teams that either very rarely or never meet face-to-face but work via information and communications technology (e-mail, telephone, internet communications, videoconferencing, etc.). Virtual teams may arise as the result of, for example, flexible working or remote site working.
Networks and communities of practice	Sharing of information. Support and development. Influence.

build mutual support, cohesion, personal relationships and interactions and is involved in the clarification of tasks and agreement of objectives.

• *Performing*: the group delivers successful performance and achievement of goals, openness, helpfulness, flexibility, co-operation and cohesion.

• *Adjourning*: as the task is completed and/or the group members move on. The role of the leader is to facilitate reflection, reassure, and ensure that the group continues to perform if it is to continue with different members and new goals.

Multiple factors impact on a team's effectiveness. These can be summarized as:

- *Establishing the purposes*: a clear definition of and understanding of the team task, coupled with a clear and agreed allocation of workload, responsibilities and authority.
- *Establishing the environment and group cohesion*: through developing norms and expectations, location, task, size, communication channels and approaches.
- *Establishing effective group structures*: group structures relate to the way in which members relate to each other. This works along several dimensions including power, status, liking, communication, role and leadership.
- *Establishing team members, the leader and groups' roles*: Belbin's team role theory is widely used. He identified nine team roles that are viewed as crucial for a well balanced and performing team. The team leader's role is to strive to create a balanced team.
- *Establishing learning*: ensuring continual reflection, development and training of all group members, to engender flexibility, willingness to change, and a learning and innovative culture.

To be effective, innovative and creative teams need to go through a development process like all other teams and their effectiveness depends on similar factors to those that impact on all other teams. But, what is different about innovative and creative teams? West (2002) suggests that the following factors determine the level of group innovation:

Task characteristics: groups or teams are typically put together to perform a specific task; the task effectively defines the team – who is in the team, what their roles are, how they should work together and the nature of the processes in which they are involved. West (2002) suggests that the task characteristics that evoke innovation are: completeness (i.e. whole tasks), varied demands, opportunities for social interaction, autonomy, opportunities for learning, development possibilities for the task and task significance.

Group knowledge diversity and skills: in successful creative teams, team members work together to link ideas from many sources, and to explore unknown areas to discover new approaches. Many authors suggest that this process is enriched by having a team comprised of people who are diverse in skills and experience (Ario, 2006). For example, Walton (2008) suggests that having a library team completely made up of creative individuals would not be productive. Bringing together people with different backgrounds, experience and personalities provides the opportunity to see issues from a variety of different perspectives and to achieve fruitful cross-fertilization of ideas. However, Taylor and Greve (2006) warn that individuals must be familiar with a knowledge domain in order to be able to push its boundaries, so the skills and knowledge of the team members are crucial, as is the team's ability to draw these out and optimize their use. Whether this opportunity is grasped and positive outcomes realized, however, depends crucially on the leadership and management of such teams. As West (2002, 355) says: 'Diversity of knowledge and skills is a powerful predictor of innovation, but integrating group processes and competencies are needed to enable the fruits of this diversity to be harvested.'

Integrating group processes: creative and innovative teams need to go through a group development process as outlined above; the focus of this is the development of group processes. West (2002) suggests that the key integrating group processes in innovation teams are:

1 *Clarifying and ensuring commitment to group objectives.*
2 *Participation in decision making*: to promote sharing of ideas, and listening and attending to the ideas of others.
3 *Managing conflict effectively*: particularly challenging with a diverse group. However, constructive controversy may improve the quality of decision making and creativity.

4 *Minority influence*: whereby it is possible for 'minorities' to be heard, and their ideas evaluated and, on occasions, adopted.
5 *Supporting innovation*: such that innovative attempts are rewarded, not punished (as discussed in Section 4.3).
6 *Developing intra-group safety*: such that group members feel safe and comfortable with each other, through encouraging a positive group affect (liking for each other and the group), constructive management of conflict, and a climate in which it is safe to be wrong, and to learn.
7 *Reflexivity*: the extent to which team members collectively reflect upon the team's objectives, strategies and processes, as well as the wider organization and market environment, and adapt accordingly.
8 *Developing group members' integration skills*: or their individual ability to work effectively in teams.

External context and its demands: the external context for the group's work, including organizational climate, support systems and market environment, is, according to West (2002), likely to impact on both the group's creativity and innovation. Taking the conventional view on the difference between creativity and innovation, i.e. that creativity is thinking about new things, while innovation implementation is about doing new things, West (2002) suggests that the external environment acts differentially on creativity and innovation. External demands inhibit creativity, but facilitate innovation. In other words, uncertainty, time constraints, competition and threat motivate groups to innovate, while many of the same demands may inhibit creativity. This may be because when a threat or constraint is perceived by the group they will pull together to innovate to resolve the situation, and may focus their efforts on implementation, rather than on the quality of their ideas. There is clearly a tension here that groups and their leaders need to resolve on an ongoing basis.

Reflect: Diversity is seen as important in innovative and creative teams. From your experience of working in diverse teams, what do you expect to be some of the challenges that diversity poses as the group progresses through the stages of group development (forming, norming, storming and performing)?

Taking a more directive stance than West, Shalley and Gilson (2004) suggest that more creative teams have the following features:

- they perceive that their tasks require high levels of creativity
- all team members share the same goals
- they value participative problem solving
- the climate is supportive of creativity.

In summary, creative and innovative teams share many of the common characteristics and development processes of other teams and groups. However, in order to be creative and innovative, they need to be committed to innovation, be able to draw on the diverse skills and knowledge of team members and others beyond the team, manage group processes to facilitate learning from each other and need to respond to the external context and its demands.

4.6 Innovation and entrepreneurship strategies

While strategy can exist without innovation, it is unlikely that effective innovation can occur without the use of strategy.

(Deiss, 2004, 17)

Leaders play a proactive role in setting direction and creating shared vision. Leaders who are seeking to promote innovation should consider the value of an innovation or entrepreneurship strategy as a public commitment to innovative and entrepreneurial behaviours at the top of the organization, and to putting innovation and entrepreneurship on the organizational agenda. A strategy identifies priorities for innovative and entrepreneurial activity, and informs the effective use of staff and other resources. In addition, a strategy is the basis for more tightly co-ordinated innovative and entrepreneurial behaviours and initiatives, communication and knowledge sharing. Finally, the review and revision of the strategy over time will allow the organization to reflect on and develop its entrepreneurial competence in a way that is relevant to the organization's mission and direction. Too many information organizations are keen to pursue exciting initiatives and good ideas, but fail to prioritize and allocate resources. Indeed, they are often in positions in which external agencies drive innovations, and the accessing of specific resources or getting involved in a new project seems like a good opportunity. The question that needs to be asked is always 'Is this the right opportunity?' Even if a formal and fully worked out innovation and entrepreneurship strategy document seems like a pipedream, some agreement as to the entrepreneurial behaviours that are welcomed and the types and extents of innovations that can be supported over a given timescale is an important step in the right direction.

Ireland, Kuratko and Morris (2006) suggest that a corporate entrepreneurship strategy can help with prioritization and more specifically with the answers to the following questions:

- Where does the organization want to be in terms of its level of entrepreneurial intensity?
- To what extent are the organization's entrepreneurial efforts orientated towards growing new businesses and starting new ventures, versus transforming the existing business?
- In what areas does the organization want to be an innovation leader versus being an innovation follower vis-à-vis its industry? In what market spaces does the firm seek to be a first mover, or a second mover?
- What is the relative importance over the next three years of product innovation versus process innovation? What is the relative importance of new versus existing markets?
- To what extent are innovation stimuli expected to come from

top, middle or first-level managers? Are all managers clear about what the organization expects from them in terms of stimulating entrepreneurial behaviour and innovations?

4.7 Launching an innovation and change management

4.7.1 Readiness

The success of an innovation depends crucially upon the political and social climate surrounding its development and launch. The social climate surrounding an innovation determines to a large extent how it will be perceived, and therefore how it will be received. Innovation is a two-way process between the innovator and their community; without social acceptance, even with a well planned and resourced innovation process, the innovation will not happen. We have discussed the concept of adoption and models of the diffusion process in Chapter 2. Here, we briefly take one step further back to emphasize the need to assess the 'readiness' of potential users and other stakeholders for an innovation.

Deiss (2004) suggests that the ability of an organization to assess 'readiness' of customers for a particular innovation is related to its ability to interpret what the customer needs and wants, and, equally importantly, to understanding the social and political climate at the point of launch or other relevant times. She also suggests that creating effective messages about the benefits of the innovation for the intended customer is an integral part of the innovation itself. In other words, as every commercial organization knows, placing an innovation into the marketplace needs an effective communication or marketing strategy. Clearly, organizations that engage their users in various ways in the innovation process (as discussed in Section 5.3) have not only incorporated valuable customer intelligence into their innovation, but already have customers who know about and hopefully are enthusiastic about an innovation. They can be a valuable catalyst in the communication process, but this is no excuse to abdicate from direct responsibility for effective and direct communication with the wider user community. In summary, successful innovations are dependent on both customer readiness and effective message conveyance.

Deiss (2004) offers an interesting example from the public library sector in the US, the introduction of self-service book check-out terminals, where both customer readiness and message conveyance were not adequately considered. The new service resulted in longer queues rather than shorter ones, was bedevilled by technical glitches, and required users to learn new roles and technology. Also, the service was launched at a time before the public was ready to 'do work for themselves', in other words before customers were accustomed to self-service. Customers could not see the benefits of the new service. Librarians could have worked with vendors on the design of the equipment, as well as observing and better understanding customer behaviour, to deliver a more beneficial innovation.

Another more recent and significant context in which 'readiness' has been a real problem is in the adoption of e-government by citizens. Public sector organizations across the globe have been investing significant resources in the development of e-government as the basis for enhanced and more efficient service delivery and increased citizen participation, but citizen adoption and use of e-government has been disappointing. Lack of citizen readiness is a key problem. Citizens are accustomed to engaging with government departments and agencies through other channels; these are familiar to them, and they have not been convinced of the need to change, even though many are avid users of the internet for other purposes (Wauters and Lorincz, 2008).

Any innovation can be viewed as a disruption to normal routines and activities. What might be perceived as a long gestation period to those promoting an innovation may be seen as a sudden change to those expected to adopt the innovation. People on the periphery of the innovation process, such as users, members of other departments possibly, for whom the innovation is intended to deliver benefits, can feel seriously inconvenienced by having to adapt to change in, for example, a service or process which they engage with only occasionally. At the very least, there is always a push–pull tension associated with the change consequent upon an innovation. The politics of innovation, or how the innovation is introduced, is very important. Considerations of the social and political context of the launch of an innovation are explored further in the next subsection, which considers the change management processes associated with the launching of an innovation.

Reflect: Can you think of any innovation where 'readiness' has been a barrier to the success of the innovation?

4.7.2 Internal markets and change management

Many process and service innovations are launched to internal customers. Such innovations may change the job roles of these internal customers, and can be very politically sensitive. Innovations can often be viewed as disruptions. Indeed, there is widespread recognition that there is a tension in organizations between sustaining existing operations and responding to the need to innovate. Wilkie (2009) discusses, for example, the change management associated with the introduction of RFID in libraries.

Successful innovators realize that not everyone may be as enthusiastic about the latest innovation as they are. As discussed earlier in this chapter, leaders and teams can take steps to enhance the innovativeness of their organization, and to seek to create organizational cultures that encourage innovation, but this will not alter the fundamental fact that innovation means change, and the change processes associated with an innovation, especially process innovations that affect people's working lives, need to be managed. Process innovations often change 'the way we do things' and therefore may be associated with fundamental cultural change that challenges people's identities, relationships and roles.

Managing organizational change is challenging because change can be perceived as threatening, painful, unnecessary and disruptive. Individuals do not always perceive change to be in their own interest, and when people cannot see the benefit of change they are likely to resist it. The factors that are likely to lead to a resistance to change include:

- *Vested interests*, and desire to protect a personally favourable status quo.
- *Fear and anxiety*, variously fuelled by lack of confidence, perceived threats, misunderstanding of the need for change and its consequences or lack of trust in managers and others.
- *Lack of clarity* concerning the purpose and nature of change leading to insecurity, uncertainty and conflicting views on the change and its outcomes and consequences.
- *Low tolerance for change*, arising from a low tolerance for ambiguity and uncertainty, and concerns about one's skills and abilities being marginalized in the changed situation.

Some of these concerns are cognitive and can be addressed by training, involvement and communication, but emotional responses, associated with, for example, fear of change or lack of confidence, are more difficult to negotiate. Wilkie (2009) suggests that people have four basic emotional needs: to feel in control; to feel valued; to feel safe; and to feel that they belong. She points out that all of these are threatened in times of change. They can be addressed through a climate in which such concerns can be aired and in which individuals can be reassured, but unfortunately, in innovation and change, the news is not always good for everyone, and innovation can lead to job losses, additional workloads and other negative outcomes. Nevertheless, it is important to minimize the negative consequences of change. Key aspects of effective change management include:

- A *clear change management strategy*, articulated by key leaders and managers, and discussed and developed by others to create ownership of a *shared vision*.

- *Communication*, to ensure that all those who have a stake in the change know what is planned, and how it will affect them. Also, communication needs to be open and two-way, so that people can express their responses and ideas, and feel that these are being given due attention.
- *Education and training*, to give individuals confidence in their contribution in the future.
- *Participation and early involvement*, to ensure that people have a sense of ownership of the change. Also, this involvement may make useful contributions to the design of the innovation.
- *Open climate*, with facilitation and support, in which individual anxieties can be explored and shared and resolved in a way that is beneficial both to the individual and the organization.

Not all resistance to change is, however, at the individual level; as discussed in earlier chapters, some organizations, particularly some in the public sector, have an in-built resistance to innovation and change. Mullins (2007) suggests that, in order to ensure operational efficiency, organizations set up defence mechanisms against change, and prefer to focus on the routine things that they know they have learned to perform well. Briefly, some of the main reasons for organizational resistance to change are:

- *Organizational cultures* which typically have a strong legacy component.
- The need to maintain *stability* and *predictability*, which is often seen as important for ensuring that large organizations work effectively.
- The *cost* of investing in new resources – change often requires resources, and organizational resources such as people, buildings and equipment are usually committed and that commitment is not easy to change.
- The effect of *past contracts or agreements* with other parties, such as suppliers and customers, which are inflexible.

- *Interdepartmental power dynamics*, and any presumed changes arising from the innovation.

Summary and conclusions

The organizational context for innovation, creativity and entrepreneurship is important. There are a number of related models seeking to describe, respectively, the components of the innovative organization, the characteristics of a work environment that supports corporate entrepreneurship or the elements of a work environment that supports creativity. Such models typically identify culture and climate as having an important role in encouraging or blocking innovation. Culture is concerned with working practices or 'the way we do things'. Key aspects of an innovative culture are support from management for new ideas, a 'we're in it together' attitude, and a commitment to striving for a reputation for innovation. Other insights can be gathered by considering the constraints on innovation in organizations.

The later sections of the chapter focus more specifically on leadership for innovation, innovative and creative teams, innovation and entrepreneurship strategies, and launching an innovation and change management. Leadership in the form of support for, and openness to, innovation is seen as critical to effective innovation. Leaders have a role both as motivators, in inspiring people, and as architects through designing an organizational environment that enables employees to be innovative. One of the roles of leaders is to develop innovative teams. Key to the success of such teams is the management of task characteristics, group knowledge diversity and skills, integrating group processes and the external context and its demands. Another of the roles of leadership is to develop and maintain a clearly articulated and co-ordinated innovation strategy. Finally, innovation will not succeed without the 'readiness' of all of those involved in the innovation. For process innovations, in particular, this means acknowledging the changes to workplaces and job roles, and using proactive change management strategies to contribute to the successful implementation of an innovation.

Review questions

1 What do you understand by the term 'innovativeness'?
2 What are the components of innovative organizations according to Bessant and Tidd (2007)? How do they compare with characteristics of a work environment that supports corporate entrepreneurship (Ireland, Kuratko and Morris, 2006)?
3 Why is culture and climate central to innovation performance in organizations?
4 How do private and public sector organizations differ in their working practices, as they relate to innovation?
5 What do you understand by a creative organization, and how does it compare with an innovative organization?
6 Discuss some of the potential barriers to, and constraints on, innovation and creativity in organizations.
7 Discuss whether transactional or transformational leadership is best suited to cultivating innovation, giving reasons as to why.
8 According to Shalley and Gilson (2004) what do leaders who seek to promote creativity focus on?
9 What are the key factors that determine the level of group innovation?
10 What contributions do corporate entrepreneurship strategies make to organizational innovation?
11 What is meant by 'readiness'? What are the potential consequences of lack of readiness to the success of an innovation?
12 Why is change management relevant to innovation in organizations? Outline some key aspects of effective change management.

Challenges

1 Can the innovativeness or innovation orientation of an organization be defined and measured?
2 What is the relative impact of the different factors that drive innovation in

organizations? Is there any dominant pattern, or does the importance of the various factors vary with the innovation and the organizational context?

3   Are some organizations better at some types of innovation, and others better at other types? If so, what leads to these differences in performance?

4   Is it more important to manage the facilitators to innovation and creativity in organizations, or to manage the barriers and constraints?

5   What leadership behaviours are most important in promoting and cultivating innovation?

6   How can teams optimize their innovative and creative outcomes?

7   How does an innovation strategy or a corporate entrepreneurship strategy fit within the overall corporate strategy of an organization? How can this process of inter-strategy fit be managed?

8   How can organizations best manage the tensions between stability and innovation?

Group discussion topics
Group discussion topic 1: Components of the innovative organization

1   Which *five* of the following components of an innovative organization would you regard as being the most important and why: shared vision, leadership, the will to innovate, appropriate organizational structure, innovative individuals, innovative teams, individual development and challenge, open communication, high level of organizational involvement in innovation, external focus, creative climate and organizational learning?

Group discussion topic 2: Innovation leadership

1   Identify two people in the library and information profession who you would describe as being innovative leaders. Why do you see these people as innovative leaders?

Group discussion topic 3: Innovative and creative teams

1 Describe the membership and task of an innovative or creative team of which you have been a member.
2 What did the team deliver that it would have been difficult for an individual to achieve?
3 Diversity is seen to be a characteristic of successful creative teams. Was this the case in the team that you describe? And what challenges did this present for group working?

References and additional reading

Advanced Institute of Management Research (2005) *Leadership for Innovation*, AIMR.

Akeroyd, J. (2000) The Management of Change in Electronic Libraries, *66th IFLA Council and General Conference 13–18 August 2000*, www.ifla.org.

Amabile, T. M., Conti, R., Coon, H., Lazenby, J. and Herron, M. (1996) Assessing the Work Environment for Creativity, *Academy of Management Journal*, **39** (5), 1154–85.

Ario, B. D. (2006) Creating Creativity, *Super Vision*, **67** (11), 11–13.

Belbin, R.M. (1981) *Management Teams: why they succeed or fail*, Heinemann

Bessant, J. and Tidd, J. (2007) *Innovation and Entrepreneurship*, Wiley.

Birkenshaw, J. and Gibson, C. (2005) *The Ambidextrous Organization*, Advanced Institute of Management Research.

Coveney, B. (2008) Assessing the Organizational Climate for Creativity in a UK Public Library Service: a case study, *Library and Information Research*, **32** (1–2), 38–56.

Cullen, J. (2007) Information Work and the Opportunity of Innovation: from corporate to social product development, *Business Information Review*, **24** (3), 156–60.

Deiss, K. J. (2004) Innovation and Strategy: risk and choice in user-centered libraries, *Library Trends*, **53** (1), 17–32.

Drucker, P. F. (1985) *Innovation and Entrepreneurship*, Heinemann.

Dunphy, D. C. and Stace, D. A. (1990) *Under New Management: Australian organizations in transition*, McGraw-Hill.

Ensor, J., Cottam, A. and Band, C. (2001) Fostering Knowledge Management through the Creative Work Environment: a portal model from the advertising industry, *Journal of Information Science*, **27** (3), 137–55.

Handy, C. (1993) *Understanding Organizations*, 4th edn, Penguin.

Harvard Business School (2003) *Managing Creativity and Innovation*, Harvard Business School.

Heye, D. (2006) Creativity and Innovation: two key characteristics of the successful 21st century information professional, *Business Information Review*, **23** (4), 252–56.

Hourston, S. (2006) Creativity and the Resilient Health Librarian, *Journal of the Canadian Health Care Libraries Association*, **27**, 35–7.

Huczynski, A. and Buchanan, D. (2007) *Organizational Behaviour: an introductory text*, 7th edn, Prentice Hall.

Ireland, R. D., Kuratko, D. F. and Morris, M. H. (2006) A Health Audit for Corporate Entrepreneurship: innovation at all levels: part 1, *Journal of Business Strategy*, **27** (1), 10–17.

Kanter, R. M. (2003) *Rosabeth Moss Kanter on the Frontiers of Management*, Harvard Business School Press.

Light, P. C. (1998) *Sustaining Innovation: creating nonprofit and governmental organizations that innovate naturally*, Jossey-Bass.

Lumpkin, G. T. and Dess, G. G. (1996) Clarifying the Entrepreneurial Orientation Construct and Linking it to Performance, *Academy of Management Review*, **21** (1), 135–72.

Lumpkin, G. T. and Dess, G. G. (2001) Linking Two Dimensions of Entrepreneurial Orientation to Firm Performance: the moderating role of environment and industry life cycle, *Journal of Business Venturing*, **16** (5), 429–51.

Martins, E. C. and Terblanches, F. (2003) Building Organizational Culture that Stimulates Creativity and Innovation, *European Journal of Innovation Management*, **6** (1), 64–74.

Moss Kanter, R. (1982) The Middle Manager as Innovator,

Harvard Business Review, **60** (4), 95–105.

Moss Kanter, R. (2002) Creating the Culture for Innovation. In Hesselbein, F., Goldsmith, M. and Somerville, I. (eds), *Leading for Innovation and Organizing for Results*, Jossey-Bass.

Moss Kanter, R. (2006) Innovation: the classic traps, *Harvard Business Review*, **84** (11), 72–83.

Mullins, L. J. (2007) *Management and Organizational Behaviour*, 8th edn, FT Prentice Hall.

Mumford, M. D., Scott, G. M., Gaddis, B. and Strange, J. M. (2002) Leading Creative People: orchestrating expertise and relationships, *The Leadership Quarterly*, **13** (6), 705–50.

Patterson, F. and Kerrin, M. (2009) *Innovation for the Recovery: enhancing innovative working practices*, Chartered Management Institute.

Paul, G. (2000) Mobilising the Potential for Initiative and Innovation by Means of Socially Competent Management, *Library Management*, **21** (2), 81–5.

Roberts, S. and Rowley, J. (2004) *Managing Information Services*, Facet Publishing.

Roberts, S. and Rowley, J. (2008) *Leadership: the challenge for the information profession*, Facet Publishing.

Schacter, D. (2005) Creative Chaos: innovation in special libraries, *Information Outlook*, **9** (12), 10–11.

Schein, E. H. (1985) *Organizational Culture and Leadership*, Jossey-Bass.

Shalley, C. E. and Gilson, L. L. (2004) What Leaders Need to Know: a review of social and contextual factors that can foster or hinder creativity, *The Leadership Quarterly*, **15** (1), 33–53.

Siguaw, J. A., Simpson, P. M. and Enz, C. A. (2006) Conceptualizing Innovation Orientation: a framework for study and integration of innovation research, *Journal of Product Innovation Management*, **23** (6), 556–74.

Stace, C. and Dunphy, D. (2001) *Beyond the Boundaries: leading and re-creating the successful enterprise*, McGraw-Hill.

Taylor, A. and Greve, H. R. (2006) Superman or the Fantastic

Four? Knowledge Combination and Experience in Innovative Teams, *Academy of Management Journal*, **49** (4), 723–40.

Tidd, J., Bessant, J. and Pavitt, K. (2005) *Managing Innovation: integrating technological, market and organizational change*, Wiley.

Tuckman, B. C. and Jensen, M. A. C. (1977) Stages of Small Group Development Revsited, *Group and Organizational Studies*, **2** (4), 419–27.

Walton, G. (2008) Theory, Research and Practice in Library Management 4: creativity, *Library Management*, **29** (1/2), 125–31.

Wauters, P. and Lorincz, B. (2008) User Satisfaction and Administrative Simplification within the Perspective of eGovernment: two faces of the same coin? *European Journal of ePractice*, **4**, www.epracticejournal.eu.

West, M. A. (2002) Sparkling Fountains or Stagnant Ponds: an integrative model of creativity and innovation implementation in work groups, *Applied Psychology: an International Review*, **51** (3), 355–424.

Wilkie, S. (2009) First, Make Sure your Staff are Involved, *Library & Information Gazette*, **5**, November, 5.

5

Innovation in practice

Learning objectives

After reading this chapter you should be able to:

* Plan an innovation strategy, taking into account the specific stages in an innovation project, including the stages of idea generation and opportunity identification, concept testing and development and implementation.
* Consider approaches to capitalizing on the potential of input from customers and users as innovators.
* Appreciate the value of, and challenges in, open innovation and collaborative innovation and the role of networks and partnerships.
* Discuss and reflect on the relationship between innovation, knowledge and learning and its consequences for the contribution of information organizations to innovation beyond the information organization.

5.1 Introduction

This chapter draws together some of the important practicalities of innovation processes in organizations. The first section, on the innovation project, revisits the idea of a stage model of innovation introduced in Chapter 2, and further develops discussion on how specific innovation projects can be facilitated, managed and led. This is followed by two sections that focus on the involvement of customers and users in innovation and on capitalizing on resources from outside the organization, through networks and partnerships. Finally, a discussion of the relationship between innovation and knowledge and learning proposes a wider agenda for the involvement of information organizations in innovation in the public sector and beyond.

5.2 The innovation project

Innovations that have the potential to make a significant impact on the organization, either in terms of business and organizational processes, or in terms of the products and services that they deliver to the marketplace, require a managed process. Such a process plays an important role in managing the allocation and deployment of resources, in sequencing and timing of activities, and in communication between all stakeholders. Chapter 2 introduced the idea of an n-step model of the innovation process, and offered three different models of the process proposed by three different authors. In practice, there is such a wide variation in types and scales of innovation, as well as in the organizational contexts in which innovation takes place, that the steps in an innovation process need to be tailored to the innovation. It is important, however, that all innovation process models embed decision points between each stage. So, for example, after idea generation, and prior to feasibility analysis, there must be a decision as to which ideas to take forward to feasibility analysis.

In this section what is proposed is not an innovation process model, but rather a discussion of elements of the innovation process that must feature in all innovation projects. These are grouped under three headings: ideas and opportunities; concept testing and development; and implementation.

5.2.1 Ideas and opportunities

There is general agreement that innovation (and entrepreneurship) commence with ideas and opportunities. But is an idea an opportunity? An idea is a creative connection between two or more pieces of information. An opportunity can only exist where there is a need, problem and an actual or potential demand for a product, service or experience. Importantly, an idea without a demand will not lead to a viable innovation. For internal process innovations, this will lead to people asking 'Why are we doing this?' Innovations without a demand or need that require user or customer adoption will languish, and affect the organization's viability and possibly its reputation. In addition, it is possible to identify needs and demand, and have some ideas about meeting them, but not be able to technically or otherwise develop a product or service to solve the problem; hence there is no opportunity. Finally, the organization has to be convinced that the innovation is worthwhile and appropriate to its mission, competencies and market aspirations.

Rae (2007) crystallizes this into the four essential features of an opportunity:

- *Demand*: there is a need, problem or potential demand to be satisfied.
- *Innovation*: there is an idea for the product, service or experience to be provided.
- *Feasibility*: the idea is technologically feasible.
- *Attractiveness*: the potential reward and the level of interest to the organization.

Another way of explaining the relationship between an idea and an opportunity is to suggest that idea generation is divergent, whereas opportunity identification, the first stage towards realization and innovation, involves exploring the opportunity in context.

So, the first stage of the innovation process focuses on the generation and valuing of ideas. The source of such ideas might vary considerably depending on the type of innovation, product or process, and the technology and expertise required to generate ideas worthy of further consideration. Table 5.1 (on page 147) summarizes a number of approaches that can be adopted to support idea generation in service innovation. Some ideas, then, will emerge from customers who have some understanding of their needs, or from employees who are in a position to evaluate an idea for a potential process innovation. In addition, outreach activities, such as engagement in digital commons that involve entering into the customer's space, are a form of intelligence-gathering activity (Li, 2006). In general, organizations need to engage proactively in environmental scanning in order to identify a 'window of opportunity'. Spotting a window of opportunity, the time window in which conditions are favourable to an innovation, is a factor in the eventual success of an innovation. In public sector organizations it is not unusual and often frustrating to the potential entrepreneur when slow decision-making processes affect the timeliness of an innovation and undermine its potential value and impact.

Windows of opportunity typically arise from three main sources, and these are likely to be the most fruitful arenas for idea-spotting:

1 **Observing trends in the organizational environment**: This involves scanning both the microenvironment and the macroenvironment. The microenvironment comprises the actors close to the organization that affect its ability to serve its customers, and includes suppliers, marketing intermediaries, customer markets, competitors and publics. The macroenvironment embraces the wider societal forces that affect the microenvironment; these include:
   — Political factors: such as new government funding and policy decisions.
   — Economic factors: such as the state of the economy, levels of disposable income, and consumer spending patterns.
   — Social factors: such as social and cultural trends, demographic changes and 'fashion'.
   — Technological factors: such as new search engine technologies, e-books and innovations in mobile technologies.
   — Environmental factors: such as sustainability agendas and the availability of natural resources.
   — Legal factors: such as new legislation relating to employment, copyright and the roles of libraries.

2 **Solving a problem**: Another approach to spotting an
opportunity is to understand the problems that people have
and seek to solve them. A number of successful commercial
ventures have started from the appreciation of a problem and a
resolve to address it. Jay Sorensen dropped a cup of coffee on
his lap because it was too hot; this led him to invent an
insulating cup sleeve, the Java Jacket. Symantec Corporation
created Norton antivirus software to rid computers of viruses,
a problem that developed as internet technology was developed
and more widely adopted. Solving a problem is also an
important opportunity identification technique in process and
service innovation. Incremental innovations designed, for
example, to make a process more efficient or a service more
responsive should be regular occurrences in organizations
committed to innovation and service excellence. Anglia Ruskin
University Library undertook a 'shopping exercise'. In pursuit
of further enhancing customer service, staff were sent to
examine customer service and physical surroundings in retail
contexts, and to use their observations to make
recommendations for improvements in the university library.

(Cefai, 2010)

3 **Finding gaps in the marketplace**: Finally, opportunities may
arise from a well honed appreciation of the microenvironment,
specifically the match between what customers or users want,
and what competitors are offering. Is there a niche segment of
users whose needs are not being met? If so, what are the
characteristics of that segment, and how might those needs be
met, and would it be possible and advantageous to the
organization to do so? Or, is there a product or service
variation (e.g. mobile access to specific internet resources) that
might be valuable to some users or customers, and which could
usefully be developed?

Bessant and Tidd (2007, 18) sum up the matter of opportunity
recognition very succinctly: 'If we are going to pick up these trigger

signals – then we need to develop some pretty extensive antennae for searching and scanning around us, and that includes some capability for looking into the future'.

Indeed, others go further and suggest that organizations need to design their internal organization in order to optimize their external knowledge sourcing, and to develop specific knowledge acquiring, generating, transferring and applying strategies to support innovation (Colombo, Rabbiosi and Reichstein, 2010). They emphasize, variously, the roles of: organizational structures, human resource management practices, cross-functional and/or transnational teams, control and communication mechanisms and motivational devices. These are coupled with links to external knowledge sources, which might include acquisitions of and alliances with innovative organizations, licenses, formal and informal co-operative links and links with talented individuals and communities of practice. The previous chapter discussed organizing for innovation in general terms. We revisit this theme later in this chapter in various sections, but specifically in Section 5.5 on knowledge, learning and innovation. The key message is that ideas for innovation do not just 'pop up by chance'; idea searching and evaluating needs to be ingrained in the culture of the innovative organization.

In seeking opportunities and associated information-gathering processes, there is an important distinction to be made between 'market-pull' and 'technology-push' innovation, particularly in the context of new product and service development. 'Market-pull' suggests that the focus in opportunity identification is with the market and its needs and gaps. This approach is generally regarded as the most appropriate for incremental innovations or product-line extensions, since customers are familiar with the product type and are able to express their preferences. However, when technology offers new opportunities to meet needs or offers experience that the customer may be unaware of, or unable to express, technology-push strategies are more appropriate. Nevertheless, even with technology-push innovations, it will be important to persuade users and customers to adopt the innovation, so the developer needs a keen eye to the 'customer' benefits of the new service, product or process.

Table 5.1 Idea generation for service innovation	
Approach	**Comment**
Surveys	Surveys are useful for developing an understanding of user needs or desires. They typically ask specific questions about service improvements to understand customer preferences, or about customer lifestyles, to understand how an innovation might benefit users.
Lead users	Inviting lead users, those who are ahead of the majority in terms of their requirements from a service, to offer their ideas for improvements.
Customer developers	Involving customers in the development and design of a new service (as discussed further in Section 5.3). This can be formalized through customer advisory panels who meet regularly to discuss needs, wants and problems that may lead to new ideas.
Competitive analysis and benchmarking	Being alert to the way in which other organizations are innovating in their service delivery, and evaluating which aspects of those innovations may have value.
Industry experts or consultants	Industry experts and consultants have an overview of potential future developments and associated service innovations.
Forecasting	Forecasting typically starts with trend analysis, focusing on, say, trends in technology, markets and society, as a basis for predicting future needs and expectations to inform service development.
Focus groups	Focus groups are a gathering of five to ten people who are selected because of their relationship to the topic under discussion. They may be customers or employees. By asking them to reflect on their experience (possibly what they do not like) of an existing service they can be encouraged to generate and assess new ideas.
Brainstorming	A brainstorming 'session' is conducted with a group of people who are expected to come up with ideas on a specific topic. The main purpose is to create an atmosphere of enthusiasm, engagement and originality which facilitates the carefree expression of ideas. 'Wacky' ideas are welcome, criticism is not permitted and the pace is fast. The focus is on creativity rather than evaluation.

Reflect: Select one of the options for idea generation listed in Table 5.1 and explain how it could be used to good effect in your organization.

5.2.2 Concept testing and development

Once a number of possible ideas towards solving a problem or capitalizing on a market opportunity have been proposed, the next stage centres on the choice of ideas to take forward, and the further development of the innovation or product concept. This stage involves a commitment of resources, and those resources have to be committed in the absence of complete knowledge about the potential for the idea(s). In other words, this commitment is subject to a high level of risk. This stage is concerned with making strategic choices. Sometimes the choice is in relation to whether or not to proceed with a major project, such as a new library building or a reconfiguration of health information services. More usually, organizations are working with a portfolio of innovations and evaluating one set of innovations against another. Key decisions need to be made about which projects to take forward, against which timescales, and how resources are to be allocated across the portfolio of innovations. A systematic approach to the selection of innovations is not only an essential part of decision making, but the evidence gathered in this process and its presentation is often important in selling or pitching the idea to various stakeholders, including funding agencies, staff and venture capitalists.

Different combinations of criteria are used to screen and assess projects for taking forward to development. Feasibility analysis is the process of determining whether an idea is viable and worth pursuing. There may be more than one stage in filtering ideas, and not all ideas that pass through the first level filter may eventually advance to implementation. When an idea is judged not to be feasible, it should be dropped or redeveloped. Feasibility analysis, then, while often emphasized as part of the idea selection process, is a recurrent process. Typically feasibility analysis involves assessment of all of product/service viability, industry/market viability, organizational viability and financial viability.

Product/service viability

Product/service viability relates to the overall appeal of the potential innovation. Establishing product/service viability is concerned with creating confidence that the product/service is what the customers want, and that the product/service will have an adequate market. Product/service viability is typically established through engagement with customers through concept testing and usability testing. Figure 5.1 summarizes the benefits of conducting a product/service feasibility analysis.

Concept testing involves showing a preliminary description (concept statement) of the product or service idea to prospective customers or users to gauge customer interest, desirability and purchase or use intent. Customers may be asked to complete a questionnaire and offer comments on how the idea can be strengthened. The aim is to validate the underlying premise of the innovation concept. On this basis, a revised concept statement is produced (see Figure 5.2) and may be shown to another group of customers in order to further develop the idea. Finally, most concept tests also ask about use or buying intentions with a view to trying to estimate future engagement or sales.

Usability testing and prototype development is undertaken if the outcome of concept testing is positive. This involves the development of a prototype model of the product. The prototype can have varying levels of sophistication but to be useful it needs to reflect as much as possible of the functionality and design of the potential innovation. Usability testing is valuable because it assesses an innovation's ease of use and the user's perception of the experience, and can provide valuable feedback to inform the product development process. This is particularly important for software and website design, where the release of beta versions of software to a group of lead users is common practice.

- Getting the product right the first time.
- An early adopter community emerges.
- Avoiding any obvious flaws in product or service design.
- Using time and capital more efficiently.
- Gaining insight into additional product and service offerings.

Figure 5.1 *Benefits of conducting a product/service feasibility analysis (based on Barringer and Ireland, 2008)*

- A description of the product or service being offered.
- The intended target market, audience or user group.
- The benefits of the product or service.
- A description of how the product or service will be positioned relative to similar products or services in the marketplace.
- A description of how the product or service will be sold, distributed or made available.

Figure 5.2 *Components of a concept statement*

Reflect: Using the bullet points in Figure 5.2 draw up a concept statement for a new service innovation for your information service.

Industry/market viability

Industry or market viability relates to the overall appeal to the market of the innovation being proposed. This stage is mainly relevant for products being launched into an external marketplace. Key issues are:

- *Industry attractiveness*: relates to the extent to which there are opportunities to achieve good financial returns and a good market share in the industry sector for the proposed innovation. Markets that are fast growing, relatively young, uncrowded, have high operating margins and are important to the customer are generally seen to be optimal; anything else is a compromise, but innovation – like many other things in life – involves compromises!
- *Market timeliness*: when launching an innovation it is necessary to choose the right time. If, as recently in the personal computer industry and in the newspaper industry, there is

consolidation towards a few large players, then opportunities for entering the market are few. Another consideration for organizations with a potentially paradigmatic innovation is whether to be first into a new market – and thereby to achieve first mover advantage. First movers can set the standard for the industry, and achieve early brand recognition and market power, but being a first mover often involves high research and development investment, and high risks. Some believe that being second into a market is more sustainable than being first, since the second organization into the market can learn from the mistakes of the first, and capitalize on growing customer interest.

• *Identifying a niche*: many innovations, and certainly those launched by smaller businesses and those new to a market sector (such as public sector organizations launching small commercial ventures), seek to launch into a market niche – a narrow group of customers with similar interests. Such a niche must be large enough to make the innovation a success, but small enough to avoid direct competition with industry leaders.

Organizational viability

Organizational viability involves assessing whether the organization has the management experience, organizational competence and resources to successfully launch the innovation. As far as management capabilities are concerned, the two most important factors are passion and enthusiasm for the innovation, and an understanding of the market and its customers. Managers who are successful innovators make good use of their professional and social networks to help to plug experience or knowledge gaps (as discussed further below). Innovation also requires a range of other resources, including office space and other space (buildings) for service delivery, and, in the case of information organizations, information resources. Key among these other resources are the skills, motivations and abilities of staff. As discussed in Chapter 4, process and service innovation often involve change for employees, so it is important to assess the current availability of staff with the competences to support the innovation, and also to assess the feasibility of developing additional competencies.

Financial viability

Financial viability focuses on the availability of financial resources to support the development of the innovation, and the overall financial attractiveness of the proposed venture. Many public sector organizations, which are risk-averse (due to the pejorative influence of public accountability), have most if not all of their financial resources already committed, and are unable to predict their income in future years, identifying the financial resources to startup an initiative, and projecting future financial profiles is difficult. Often innovation is only possible when governments announce special funding initiatives. Notwithstanding, the following short checklist of factors is a useful guide to consideration of the financial viability of an innovation:

- the amount of capital invested
- the return (in financial and other terms) anticipated and the time period over which this will be achieved
- the risks assumed in launching the innovation
- the alternative uses for the money (and other resources) being invested in the innovation
- the alternative uses for the innovator's and manager's time and efforts.

Reflect: Think of an innovation with which your organization has been involved. What factors were considered either in deciding whether a major innovation would go ahead, or in selecting between competing innovation projects?

5.2.3 Implementation

Implementation is the stage of the innovation process that involves the most significant commitment of resources. As discussed in Chapter 2, implementation is concerned with making the innovation happen, by growing the innovation concept through the various stages of development to final launch. This process involves gathering, co-ordinating and managing resources, including knowledge, people, time and finance. In this process project management is important, but the unique feature of the innovation project is that the process is conducted against a backdrop of uncertainty. It is difficult to predict whether the innovation will work; there may be problems at the development stage (technological or otherwise) and, once the innovation has been developed, there may be difficulties with any of launch, marketing or adoption. So, although this section commences with a short sub-section on project management, it is important to appreciate that there are a number of factors that contribute to innovation project success, as discussed below, and as summarized in Table 5.2.

Project management

Project management is concerned with the planning, scheduling and controlling of those activities that must be performed to achieve project objectives. More specifically, project management involves:

- Putting in place an effective temporary organization to implement, manage, control and direct the project.
- Planning the activities so that outputs are produced to the required quality, on schedule and within budget.
- Managing risk to ensure that opportunities and benefits are fully evaluated.
- Managing benefits to make sure that the investment in the project makes an optimum contribution to improved performance.

- Controlling the project to make sure that the right resources are committed at the right place and right time.
- Bringing together the main interest groups and encouraging their participation.

The tasks that typically fall to the project manager are:

- *Estimation*: identifying the work and activities needed.
- *Resource allocation*: identifying who has the skills to do the work and the time to complete it.
- *Scheduling*: planning which tasks are to be completed when.
- *Budgeting*: managing and controlling costs and expenditure.
- *Monitoring and control*: ensuring that the project is progressing and that each stage is completed to schedule.

Reflect: It is likely that your organization manages some innovations explicitly as projects and that others are 'just expected to happen'. How does your organization select innovations for management as projects?

Achieving innovation project success

A successful innovation project would generally be viewed as a project which leads to a widely adopted and well accepted new product or service, or a process that introduces efficiencies and enhanced effectiveness. However, it is important to recognize that an innovation process that is abandoned before the innovation is implemented can also be viewed as a success; it is better to cut your losses and avoid further investment in an innovation that is not going to deliver, than to persist and squander more resources. Also, every innovation project is an opportunity for learning, and, provided that it is not too expensive an opportunity, may generate valuable insights, competencies, knowledge and networks that may provide the foundation for a later innovation.

Table 5.2 offers a summary of some of the key contributors to achieving innovation project success, and some of the mechanisms that can be used to support the key contributors. Table 5.2 revisits many of the issues that have been discussed in other parts of this book and, in particular, serves to emphasize that many of the topics discussed in Chapter 4, such as innovation teams, an innovative culture and leadership, are key contributors to innovation success.

Table 5.2 *Achieving innovation project success (developed from Bessant and Tidd, 2007, 426)*

Key contributors to success	Associated mechanisms
Systematic process for progressing innovations	Innovation process model, with identified decision points. Management and monitoring of each stage and its outcomes.
Early involvement of all relevant functions	Identification of key internal stakeholders. Establishment of effective internal and external communication mechanisms.
Overlapping/ parallel working	Concurrent or simultaneous development from different functions and teams in order to achieve faster development, project momentum and continued buy-in and commitment.
Appropriate project management structures	Structure chosen to suit innovation project and organization, e.g. line/matrix/project. Clearly identified responsibilities and roles.
Cross-functional team working	Careful selection of team members. Team-building approaches and attention to effective team working.
Advanced, computer-based support tools	Design tools, such as computer-aided design (CAD), and rapid prototyping tools. Computer-supported co-operative working tools, to support co-operative writing and design.
Innovative culture valuing learning and continuous improvement	Leadership style. Commitment to learning, and tolerance of mistakes.

Reflect: With reference to Table 5.2 rate your information organization on a scale of 1 to 5 (1 = low; 5 = high) on each of the key contributors to success for innovation.

5.3 Capitalizing on customer/user innovation

Innovation is concerned with value creation, and in the context of public sector and non-governmental organizations is about creating social and/or public value. Intending information innovators would do well to remind themselves regularly that 'The ultimate purpose of innovation is not to win awards, boost public confidence, or attract foundation support, but to create public value' (Light, 1998, xv).

This process of creating public value is and has always been a partnership. In the next section we discuss innovation through partnerships with other organizations; partnerships and alliances are an important feature of innovation in the public sector. First, however, we discuss user and customer involvement in the innovation process.

While organizations generally understand the need to listen to the customer and incorporate their perceptions of value for the customer into their innovation activities, traditional models of the innovation process tend to view customers as passive recipients or adopters of the organization's innovation activities. More recently, there has been a growing interest in engaging customers in innovation processes founded in recognition of the value of seeking to capitalize on customer knowledge developed from customers' experiences. Customer engagement in innovation, often referred to as co-production or co-creation, has a number of potential benefits, including:

1 The creation of more original and valuable ideas (Kristensson, Gustafsson and Archer, 2004).
2 Enhancement of new product development performance (Hsieh and Chen, 2005).
3 Proactive learning about the customer and the development of improved understanding of their latent needs (Dahlsten, 2004).

There are various examples of information organizations engaging users in service improvement. These include:

• Using high school pupils to help in the design of a dedicated space for children aged 11 to 18 at a public library.

- Using volunteers to catalogue books online for a specialist local archaeology and history library.

We discuss customer involvement in innovation further through the exploration of two key themes: lead users and customer co-creation.

5.3.1 Lead users

Von Hippel proposes the idea of the democratization of innovation – the shift in power to the user – which to libraries and other organizations in the information industry is ever present:

> When I say that innovation is being democratized, I mean that users of products and service – both firms and individuals – are increasingly able to innovate for themselves . . . . Users that innovate can develop exactly what they want, rather than relying on manufacturers to act as their (often very imperfect) agents. Moreover, individual users do not have to develop everything they need on their own: they can benefit from innovation developed and freely shared by others.
>
> (Von Hippel, 2005, 1)

Cullen (2007) offers an extreme example of user involvement in the innovation process. He suggests that Shawn Fanning did the music industry a big favour, and certainly precipitated a paradigm innovation, by demonstrating through Napster that music lovers preferred managing their music collections digitally and acquiring music over the internet to the retail distribution options that had been previously available to them. Apple, a company with a reputation for innovation and creativity, responded by developing their iPod and iTunes products, and others have followed with the development of competitive products.

Some while ago, Von Hippel (1986) proposed the concept of 'lead users'. Lead users are those members of a user population who:

- are at the leading edge of an important market trend, and so experience needs earlier than others
- anticipate relatively high benefits from obtaining a solution to their needs
- have sufficient insights, experience and competence to identify and contribute to the development of an innovation
- are perceived to be pioneering and innovative by their peer group, such that others look to follow their example.

Lead users (whether they be individuals or organizations) often have a keen interest in and involvement with the products that they use and may seek to customize or develop them to better suit their own purposes. Software suppliers often work with users in this way. For example, a small software company creating educational software for use in schools works closely with the staff in a number of schools in which their software is in operation, evolving the software on the basis of intelligence gathered from lead users on problems, new government reporting initiatives for schools and competitor product development (Jones and Rowley, 2010). Morrison, Roberts and Von Hippel (2000) discuss lead users' involvement in the modification of Online Public Access Catalog (OPAC) information search systems in Australia. They discovered that 26% of libraries using OPACs modified the system to suit local circumstances. Lead users were those with 'leading-edge status' and good in-house technical capabilities. Lead users were typically also enthusiastic to share their innovations with others. Bragge, Tuunanen and Marttiin (2009) discuss the value of virtual communities in engaging lead users in information systems development.

Lead users have a number of potential roles in innovation; they:

- Contribute to the organization's awareness of evolving customer needs and requirements, and act as a source of competitor and market intelligence.
- Develop their own innovations and share them with the

organization, or participate in co-development and early adoption of the innovation, in expectation of creating mutual benefits.

- Act as advocates for the organization and its services and products, building visibility and reputation for the organization, while also offering insights into the potential diffusion of the innovation.

Reflect: Are you a lead user in any arena? How might you benefit from participation in an innovation process?

5.3.2 Customer co-creation

Successful customer co-creation depends on the organization developing appropriate mechanisms and processes to facilitate and generate mutual benefits from customer involvement in co-creation. Desouza et al. (2008) suggest that a transition from older models of low or no customer involvement requires attention to the different types of customer innovation, organizational mission and organizational structure.

The concept of co-creation of value is central to debates about the nature of marketing and service delivery. The dominant perspective here is that value is embedded in personal experiences, and that the customer can be granted different levels of control in designing their own experiences. Indeed, Prahalad and Ramaswamy (2000) suggest that the locus of innovation and co-production is shifting from products and services to the 'experience environment'. Accordingly, customers are at the very least continuously engaged in interpreting and shaping the service context created by the service supplier, and thereby participating in innovation. This perspective has particular resonance for information service delivery in digital contexts in which the information searcher and user has been empowered by both search and social networking technologies.

Payne, Storbacka and Frow (2008) offer a thought-provoking list of five different kinds of contexts in which the customer is engaged in co-creation:

1 *Emotional management of the customer* through advertising and promotional activities.
2 *Self-service*, where there is a transfer of labour to the customer.
3 The supplier provides the experience and the *customer is part of the context* (e.g. Disney Theme Parks, where the customer is assigned a role to act out).
4 The *customer self-selects*, using the supplier's prescribed processes, to solve their particular problem, as in when, for instance, a user selects the opportunities offered by a website to complete a task, or create an experience that generates value for them.
5 The customer and supplier engage in the *co-design of new products and services*.

Co-creation can be viewed as an aspect of customer knowledge management (CKM), the process through which organizations seek to 'know what their customers know'. Gibbert, Leibold and Probst define customer knowledge management as:

> The strategic process by which cutting edge companies emancipate their customers from passive recipients of products and service, to empowerment as knowledge partners. CKM is about gaining, sharing, and expanding the knowledge residing in customers, to both customer and corporate benefit.
>
> (Gibbert, Leibold and Probst, 2002, 460)

Customer knowledge management, then, changes the emphasis from collecting data and information in order to learn about customers, to learning with customers. Such customers may be either individual consumers or users, or partner organizations. Gibbert, Leibold and Probst (2002) discuss five different styles of customer knowledge management:

1 *Prosumerism*: where the customer fulfils the dual role of producer and customer.
2 *Team-based co-learning*: where corporate social capital is generated through team learning, across the value chain (with business customers).
3 *Mutual innovation*: where organizations and their lead users work together to create innovations that are beneficial to all parties.
4 *Communities of creation*: where groups of people work together over a long period of time, have shared interests, and want to jointly create and share knowledge.
5 *Joint intellectual property*: where the organization is 'owned' by its customers, and the intellectual property does not reside in the organization but is partly 'owned' by the customers, and customer success becomes organization success and vice versa.

These processes are variously discussed further in Section 5.3.3. on community co-creation and in Section 5.4 on collaborative and open innovation.

Reflect: Select one of the above types of CKM and consider how it might usefully be implemented in your information organization.

5.3.3 Community co-creation

The internet can be a valuable platform for customer engagement in innovation, due to its interactivity, enhanced reach, persistence, speed and flexibility. Particularly attractive is the opportunity that internet-based tools offer for engaging not just with individual customers, but with customer communities. Sawhney, Verona and Prandelli (2005) summarize some key internet-based collaboration mechanisms, and map them on the basis of the nature of collaboration and stage of the new product development process, as shown in Figure 5.3. High richness mechanisms are those that emphasize the generation of ideas and insights,

Nature of collaboration		Applicability to stage of innovation process	
		Developing Ideas and Concepts	Innovation Design and Testing
	Deep/High Richness	Suggestion box. Advisory panels. Virtual communities. Web-based idea markets. Information pump.	Toolkits for user innovation. Open-source mechanisms. Web-based patent markets.
	Broad/High Reach	Online survey. Market intelligence services\web-based conjoint analysis. Listening-in techniques.	Mass customization of the product. Web-based prototyping. Virtual product testing. Virtual market testing.

Figure 5.3 *Mapping internet-based collaboration mechanisms based on nature of collaboration (adapted from Sawhney, Verona and Prandelli, 2005)*

whereas high reach mechanisms encourage engagement with larger numbers of customers, which can be useful in gauging responses to proposals and ideas across a representative sample of potential users. In addition, different mechanisms are more or less effective at different stages in the innovation process. The selection of internet mechanism for customer co-creation, then, has implications for the type of innovation in which customers are invited to participate.

One arena for customer engagement via the internet is virtual communities, online communities, and the communities associated with social networking sites. Such communities bring together users who have common interests to share their experiences and knowledge, and are a rich source of socially generated knowledge (Wenger, 2000). They often have a high level of involvement with the focus of the community, and even specific and relevant technical competencies (as, for example, with a community of video game enthusiasts, or open-source software developers).

Virtual customer communities enable organizations to establish distributed innovation models that involve varied customer roles in innovation and new product development. In the information sector there has been much discussion of the role of members of such communities in the creation of content, ranging from software, through music, social experiences, images, moving images, learning objects and scholarly articles.

An interesting example of an innovation community in the information profession is the Juice Project. The Juice Project is an open-source project hosted on its own website and backed by the Google Code repository, and supported by Talis. The Juice Project seeks to make code developed by a range of innovators working in different libraries easy to integrate into any library OPAC, in order to enhance its functionality and the user experience (Wallis, 2009).

For online communities to be a successful source of innovation for an organization, the organization needs to cultivate engagement in and contribution to the community, using a combination of intangible incentives such as acknowledgement of status or opinion leadership and tangible incentives in the form of payments. They also need to understand and, where appropriate, manage interaction patterns, knowledge creation and the integration of the virtual community with the innovation team (Nambisan, 2002). Indeed, the optimal stance for the organization seeking to work with a customer community in innovation may be that of 'customer community leadership' (Rowley, Kupiec-Teahan and Leeming, 2007). In a case study described by Rowley, Kupiec-Teahan and Leeming (2007), the innovative and interesting products created by a kite surfing company act as a catalyst around which a community gathers through the medium of the 'experience' that the products deliver. The customer community comprises those who have participated in the experiences, enjoyed them and wish to develop the interaction. Customers work in partnership with the company to build excitement and develop skill, and, by sharing experiences with others, add to the totality of the customer community. Customer community leadership for innovation has similar characteristics to innovation in other contexts. Specifically, it involves creating, sharing, communicating vision, shaping culture, developing others, building successful relationships and taking a holistic perspective (see Section 4.4).

Reflect: Does your information organization have a customer community, the members of which interact with one another towards enhancing their mutual experience of your service and proactively informing service developments and innovation? What benefits does this generate?

5.4 Collaborative and open innovation through networks and partnerships

As discussed in Chapter 4, innovation involves teams. Sometimes the team members involved in innovation are employed by different organizations. This type of innovation bridges organizational boundaries and is described as open innovation or collaborative innovation, and the groups of people who come together to progress such interorganizational innovations are referred to as innovation networks. There is a widespread recognition that the increasing complexity of and change in organizational environments drives the imperative for collaborative innovation (Ketchen, Ireland and Snow, 2007). Organizations need to build close relationships not only with customers, but also with other organizations in their supply chain and beyond. The following quote from Ketchen, Ireland and Snow seems particularly apposite for information organizations:

> Accelerating trends in globalization and information technology have helped create competitive arenas whose demands are growing quickly and unpredictably, and competition in such settings exceeds the ability to keep pace of even the most agile individual, small businesses, and corporate research and development units.
>
> (Ketchen, Ireland and Snow, 2007, 375)

Collaborative innovation is defined as the creation of innovations across firm (and perhaps industry) boundaries through the sharing of ideas, knowledge, expertise and opportunities (Miles, Miles and Snow, 2005).

Information organizations in the public sector (including public libraries, academic libraries and health libraries) have a long tradition of co-operation within the library sector in areas associated with, for example, the creation of metadata, the development of standards, consortia licensing agreements for e-journals and other digital resources, performance enhancement and benchmarking and service delivery. For example, there is currently recognition from the Society of College, National and University Libraries (SCONUL) that, in the face of expected budget cuts, coupled with a need to continue to innovate, investment in change will largely be found through partnerships and collaborations between universities, their libraries and other services. Further, Woodward and Estelle (2009) argue that libraries and publishers must collaborate to avoid the collapse of the research publishing infrastructure. In addition, national and public libraries, especially, often work in partnership with other public sector departments, agencies and services on projects associated with, for example, promoting reading and learning, developing digital literacy and variously contributing to cultural engagement in their communities. However, the need to hone their competencies in partnerships and collaborative innovation has never been greater. In particular, it is important to understand that collaboration is philosophically different from co-operation. In co-operation desired outcomes are relatively clear, the distribution of future returns and mutual benefits can be identified and negotiated in advance, and the co-operating parties act essentially in their own interest (Miles, Miles and Snow, 2005). Collaboration, on the other hand, often involves unpredictable outcomes and, as such, trust, honesty and equity are pivotal, with collaborating parties committing to understanding and taking into account one another's interests as well as their own (Von Krogh, 1998).

In professions, professional bodies, such as the Chartered Institute of Library and Information Professionals (CILIP), often play a central role in bringing partners together in order to achieve innovation that will contribute to the sector as a whole. For example, CILIP recently launched Encompass, a positive action trainee scheme to encourage black and minority ethnic community members to choose a career in library and information work. The scheme was developed by CILIP in collaboration with the skills development agency, Path National, and piloted through collaboration with the London Borough of Lewisham, the National Institute of Medical Research, the House of Commons and the House of Lords. Another innovative project uses prison labour to digitize old broadcast footage and to code documents and images. The pilot scheme, supported by the British Library and the National Archives, is taking place at the Serco-run Lowdham Grange prison, and also has the involvement of a large UK broadcaster.

In addition, many of the emerging technologies associated with Web 2.0 which support collaboration have the potential to enhance collaboration between organizations and between organizations and their lead users (Li, 2009).

The philosophy underlying open innovation is that by opening up their innovation processes, searching beyond their boundaries and developing and managing a rich set of network relationships, organizations enhance their capacity to innovate. It is widely recognized that talking to and working with people in different organizations can widen horizons, challenge assumptions and in general facilitate innovation and creativity. Typically, in open innovation there is a mutual exchange of benefits arising from:

- bringing together different and complementary knowledge and skills sets
- enhancing capacity for creativity and problem solving by enlisting more minds
- sharing of and reduction in the risks associated with exploring and exploiting new ideas, through sharing knowledge, skills and costs
- access to new markets and technologies
- shared learning and understanding, which may form a platform for future innovation.

Reflect: Choose a collaborative innovation project known to you – what benefits did the various parties derive from the collaboration?

5.4.1 Types of innovation networks

The exact benefits achieved through open and collaborative innovation will depend on the nature of the innovation network, the knowledge and skills of the member organizations and the core driver in coming together. Those types that are most likely to be relevant to information organizations include:

- *Spatial clusters*: networks which form because the members are geographically close to one another and have a mutual interest in promoting the economic, social and cultural development of their city or region. Typically, such networks involve partners from both the public and private sectors.
- *Sectoral networks*: networks which form because members perceive themselves to be in the same industry sector, and see collaboration and benchmarking as important for innovation, performance and reputation building in political arenas for the sector.
- *Sectoral consortia*: networks which form to progress a specific innovation project, possibly provoked by a government policy initiative or funding opportunity.
- *Standards forums*: networks which form around the establishment and maintenance of standards, such as those associated with new technologies, metadata and licensing.
- *New technology development networks*: networks which form because the members (either individuals or organizations) are keen to share and learn about new emerging technologies and their applications.
- *Communities of practice*: networks of individuals which are informal, often across departments and organizations, and which form because those individuals have a shared interest and find it mutually beneficial to share their knowledge and to

learn from each other. Members build relationships and trust through regular interaction, and may develop shared resources, such as tools and knowledge repositories.

Reflect: Suggest examples of each of the different types of innovation networks in the information sector.

5.4.2 Key issues in establishing and managing an innovation network

Some networks may be long standing, and have other purposes in addition to innovation. In other instances, organizations or individuals will come together in response to a specific problem or opportunity. Nevertheless, in order to be successful all innovation networks need commitment and management. They are, for example, likely to go through similar group formation stages to those experienced by internal innovation teams. However, in addition, the individuals in the network will have a keen sense of their responsibility and allegiance to their employing organization. Table 5.3 offers a checklist of the key issues that typically need to be addressed in managing an innovation network.

The relative similarity of the organizations in networks typically impacts on the levels of innovation and creativity that a network achieves. For example, networks composed of tightly coupled organizations that possess similar experiences and cultures are likely to be prone to relatively low levels of innovation (Ketchen, Ireland and Snow, 2007). Bessant and Tidd (2007) also suggest that innovation networks can be categorized on the basis of the type of innovation (incremental or radical), and on the similarity of the participating organizations, as shown in Figure 5.4, and this has consequences for the management of the innovation network. In Zone 1 innovation networks, organizations have a broadly similar background and context and are concerned with improving existing practice. As such it is important that they share experiences, disclose information, develop trust and transparency, and build a

Table 5.3 *Key issues in managing an innovation network*

Key issue	Comment
The purpose of the network	The innovation network may have an ongoing purpose towards innovation in a sector, for example, or may be formed to execute a specific project. Without a clear purpose to which members can commit the network will fall apart.
Network membership and boundaries	Network membership needs to be clearly defined and maintained. Agreed conventions are needed for changes and substitutions, and all organizations involved need to be and remain fully committed.
Decision making	Decision-making processes and protocols need to be agreed, including the process, who is involved and what records are maintained.
Conflict resolution	Different network members will have different interests and will seek different benefits from participation in the network. Success is critically dependent on negotiating towards a win–win situation for all concerned.
Communication	Communication processes and channels, their various purposes, and the level of openness and confidentiality are an important aspect of building relationships and trust.
Knowledge management	Attention needs to be directed towards how knowledge is created, captured and shared across the network.
Member participation	Networks will not work without participation; members need to be motivated to participate. Often members have different levels of participation, from full membership, through peripheral membership to passive membership. Different levels of contribution may be required from different members at different times, but they must be willing to make the contribution required of them.
Risk/benefit sharing	Managing perceptions of the distribution of risks and benefits across the network is crucial to motivation, participation and success.
Co-ordination and organization	Networks need organization and co-ordination. Members need to understand how the network objectives are to be achieved (plans, budgets, time scales) and their own and others' roles in achieving those objectives.
Leadership	Networks, like all innovative organizations, need leadership. An individual or a group needs to be granted the authority to resolve issues and conflicts that may endanger the achievement of the network's strategic objectives.

Radical innovation agenda	Zone 2 (e.g. sectoral consortia)	Zone 3 (e.g. new technology development networks)
Incremental innovation agenda	Zone 1 (e.g. sectoral networks)	Zone 4 (e.g. spatial clusters)
	Similar organizations	Heterogeneous organizations

Figure 5.4 *Types of innovation network (adapted from Bessant and Tidd, 2007)*

shared sense of commitment to innovation. While superficially relatively straightforward because the focus is incremental innovation, Chapman and Corso (2005) suggest that to sustain such collaboration is challenging because it involves an alignment of organizational processes, and extends beyond selected innovation teams to other members of the organization. An example of a Zone 1 network might be a group of academic libraries working towards improvements in their digital service delivery. Zone 2 networks, on the other hand, are working towards a radical innovation associated with new products, service or processes, and possibly capitalizing on the opportunities offered by new technologies. An example might be public libraries working together with publishers and others to establish the principles and associated business models for digital rights management for e-books. In Zone 4, the participating organizations are very different from one another, and may need to spend some time understanding each other's agendas, surfacing any potential conflicts and developing trust. An example might be a regional cluster working together to gradually build the infrastructure associated with a knowledge city. They will need to make careful judgements about what to reveal and share. Finally, Zone 3 networks are likely to involve members from different sectors, such as those in a supply chain, and are likely to bring different perspectives on the priorities in the innovation process. An example of such a network might be a strategic alliance formed by a book publisher, a search engine organization and a national library to provide access to e-books.

5.4.3 The organization perspective on open innovation

Organizations that engage in collaborative or open innovation need to develop the capabilities, structures and processes to support their engagement in collaboration. They need to take a strategic approach to innovation, co-ordinating and aligning their engagement in collaboration towards a strategic objective. Strategy and leadership is arguably even more important in collaborative innovation than in innovation within the organization (and there are at least as many things that can go wrong!). Nokia's approach to collaboration is interesting. Nokia has a network of over 300 small high-tech firms. Nokia and its partners have developed the capacity to create 'fast trust' among interacting parties in order to facilitate rapid innovation. Organizationally, Nokia can be viewed as a firm embedded in an ecosystem of flexible collaborative networks. In such an ecosystem, a lead organization can participate in many networks, each of which has the potential to drive innovation, and, in addition, there may be particular benefits to be achieved from the synergies that the organization can derive from the sum of their engagement in such networks (Ketchen, Ireland and Snow, 2007).

Since many open innovation initiatives relate to radical innovations, such as those in Zones 2 and 3, innovation projects are typically largely enacted through open innovation teams. Open innovation teams, comprised of people from different organizations, have the organizational diversity which can positively influence collaborative knowledge creation and idea generation, but can also obstruct the process. Collaboration can make the development more complicated and costly, and slower. The diversity of the team may be a basis for political and personal conflicts, which in turn lead to project failures (Du Chatenier et al., 2009).

According to Swink (2006), there are four categories of barriers to successful open innovation:

1 *Physical and temporal barriers*: Physical and temporal barriers can impede communication between team members. While

information technology solutions can facilitate communication, they cannot resolve issues such as lack of trust or ineffective goal setting (Chapman and Corso, 2005). There is a need to encourage unstructured and informal interactions between team members alongside more formal communication, which is timely; this is often most effectively achieved through physical co-location of the team.

2 *Organizational and hierarchical barriers*: Teams can easily be hampered by standard operating procedures, organizational structures and budget controls. A separate organization for the project, with its own people and other resources, is one way to give the team the necessary autonomy. In addition, it may be necessary to realign reporting relationships, and support team members in negotiating conflicts between their allegiance to a functional or previous team and their allegiance to the project.

3 *Relational and cultural barriers*: Individual team members bring 'baggage' to their role in the team. They may be unwilling to collaborate or participate as a team member, due to perceived loss of power or status, or lack of interest or motivation. They may view being moved to a project team as being sidelined, especially if this reduces their opportunities for working with established and trusted colleagues within the organization. They may perceive their involvement in an innovation project that may or may not work as personally risky. Further, while having the requisite technical skills to contribute to the project, they may feel uncomfortable with the rather different experience and culture of the innovation team. All of these potential barriers need to be managed.

4 *Knowledge, information and data management systems-related barriers*: The effectiveness of collaborative teams can be considerably hindered by the need for rapid development of technologies to support communication and appropriate levels of access to data and information. Added to this is the need to continually judge what data and information can be shared with people outside the organization, without compromising

confidentiality or competitiveness. Finally, there is the issue that many processes, values and approaches within organizations, which may be the foundation for the innovation, are not recorded, and frequently organizations need to spend time and resources developing the knowledge of the how and why of their processes, before it can be shared with others.

Du Chatenier et al. (2009) develop a more elaborate model of the factors that need to be managed towards collaborative knowledge creation in open innovation teams, and cluster factors into three groups associated, respectively, with team emergent states, team composition inputs and team-level inputs. While this model reiterates a number of the issues discussed in Chapter 4 on innovation teams, this would be worthwhile further reading for those engaged in collaborative innovation.

5.5 Knowledge, learning and innovation

Information professionals need to understand and be active proponents of innovation not only for the benefit of their own organizations, but also for the contribution that they can make through supporting knowledge acquisition and creation and learning in other organizations, and for communities and societies. Contributing to innovation in contexts beyond the information organization may be achieved through participation in open innovation and innovation networks, as discussed in the previous section, or through the more general facilitation of innovation and creativity through the provision of advice and information and the development of innovation hubs. For example, the National Library of Scotland (2004) identified public libraries as crucibles for innovation and creativity. Similarly, other commentators argue for the role of the public library in promoting creativity and innovation in their communities (e.g. Nijboer, 2006). Equally importantly, there is plenty of evidence that, with advances in technology and changing organizational landscapes, information professionals have needed to adapt and change, and in this process many have engaged and developed their creativity and developed and implemented innovation. Information professionals have, of necessity, become experienced innovators.

This section seeks to cultivate further reflection on the wider role of information professionals in innovation.

5.5.1 The traditional perspective

Heye (2006) offers a useful list of some of the ways in which information professionals can help their organizations in supporting innovation. These include:

1 dissemination of information; locating internal and external information relevant to innovation for the organization, extracting and distilling the key messages, and delivering this to the key groups involved in innovation
2 provision of access to books, journals and electronic resources both to support specific innovation activities and to encourage reflection on innovation processes, practices and management
3 acting as a hub for innovation information, through use of external networks
4 acting as creativity facilitators, organizing creativity seminars and workshops.

With the ever-increasing development of information retrieval and management tools and access to increasingly rich sets of digital data and other resources, innovation teams will benefit from support not only in gathering information, but also in ensuring that they are making optimal use of the tools, data and information available.

5.5.2 Knowledge management and innovation

While Heye (2006) writes as an information professional seeking to cultivate more discussion about innovation in the information profession, many writers in the management field also recognize and discuss the issue of the relationship between an organization's knowledge management strategies and practices and its innovation performance. There is widespread recognition that effective knowledge management (KM) is a precursor to successful innovation (Amabile et al., 1996; Hull, Coombs and Peltu, 2000; Sonderquist, Chanaron and Motwani, 1997), and that 'the process of innovation depends heavily on knowledge' (Gloet and Terziovski, 2004, 402). Knowledge management is concerned with obtaining and communicating ideas and information that underpin innovation competencies. The key contribution of KM to innovation lies in three areas (Adams, Bessant and Phelps, 2006):

• idea generation (as discussed earlier in this chapter)
• knowledge repository creation and access (embracing both implicit and explicit knowledge)
• information flow (such as information gathering and networking).

In considering the role of KM in innovation, it is important to understand that knowledge is more than data or information, and knowledge management involves more than information management. Knowledge is information combined with experience, context, interpretation and reflection (Davenport, De Long and Beers, 1998), and knowledge management covers the management of explicit and implicit knowledge held by the organization (Nonaka, 1991). Coleman (1999) defines KM as an umbrella term for a wide variety of interdependent and interlocking functions consisting of: knowledge creating; knowledge valuation and metrics; knowledge mapping and indexing; knowledge transport, storage and distribution; and knowledge sharing. Developing from this, Beckman (1999) makes the link between KM and innovation. He views KM as being concerned with the formalization of and access to experience, knowledge and expertise which creates new capabilities, enables superior performance, encourages innovation and enhances customer value.

There is a growing body of evidence to suggest that successful KM is dependent upon both effective implementation and management of information and communication technology (ICT) infrastructures (to support access to data and information, and communication), and a focus on people, centred on learning, skills and competencies (e.g. Gloet and Terziovski, 2004). Successful organizations learn how to create knowledge policies, processes and cultures that work for them. For innovation, it is essential that organizations have a high level of competence in combining new and existing knowledge. The concept of 'absorptive capacity' refers to the organization's ability to absorb and put to use new knowledge, which depends on their ability to recognize the value and relevance of new, external knowledge, assimilate it, and apply it in order to develop successful innovations (Cohen and Levinthal, 1990). Higher levels of absorptive capacity are positively related to innovation and organizational performance (Chen, 2004).

Dasgupta and Gupta (2009) represent the links between structure, culture, technology, leadership, organizational learning, knowledge management, innovation process and innovation outcome, effectively as shown in the adaption of their diagram in Figure 5.5. They suggest that the ability of organizations to differentiate themselves, and thereby to survive and flourish, depends on how efficiently they integrate their innovation management practices with their knowledge management practices so as to harness knowledge for innovation.

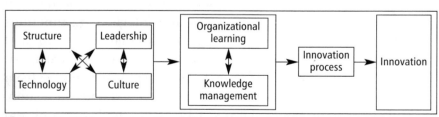

Figure 5.5 *Linking organizational characteristics, learning, knowledge and innovation*

5.5.3 Extending the information professional's role in innovation

There are potentially a wide range of different types of contributions that information and knowledge managers can make to innovation. These include:

1 assisting in creating tools, platforms and processes to support the tacit knowledge creation, sharing and leverage that is central to innovation

2 assisting in converting tacit knowledge to explicit knowledge, through discussion databases and online communities of practice

3 facilitating collaboration and the flow of knowledge in the innovation process across functional boundaries within organizations, and also across organizational boundaries through online collaboration forums, and intranets and extranets

4 ensuring the availability and accessibility of both tacit and explicit knowledge used in the innovation process, and the integration of the organization's knowledge base, using knowledge organization and retrieval skills and tools

5 assisting in identifying gaps in the knowledge base and providing processes to fill the gaps

6 assisting in the steady development of the knowledge base through gathering and capturing tacit and explicit knowledge

7 contributing to the cultivation of a knowledge-driven culture for the incubation of innovations.

(based on Du Plessis, 2007)

Coulson-Thomas (2004, 85) argues that: 'knowledge management should be an end-to-end process from identifying knowledge requirements and gaps, through the creation, packaging and sharing of knowledge to its application to enable innovation'. In this statement he is both arguing that the outcome of knowledge management is innovation, and also emphasizing the need to go through all of the knowledge management processes in order to arrive at that endpoint. Information and knowledge professionals can become over preoccupied with the middle, knowledge sharing and dissemination stages of the process, with a danger that insufficient attention will be focused on knowledge creation and exploitation. Indeed, there is some tentative evidence that knowledge dissemination and codifying knowledge in databases and other organizational memories does not contribute to innovation (e.g. Darroch and McNaughton, 2002; Tang, 1999), and that the most important contributors to innovation are knowledge acquisition and responsiveness to knowledge. In other words, information professionals need to extend their role beyond knowledge collection, storage and dissemination to creating new social knowledge about the potential for cross-silo alliances. Cullen (2007) argues that, since information services often exist outside the silo-based political manoeuvring in organizations, industrial information services, in particular, are an important apolitical node for gathering information and for suggesting and facilitating alliances that otherwise would not have happened. In this role, the communicative ability of information professionals is pivotal.

Individuals, teams, organizations and communities innovate by creating and exploiting new knowledge; information and knowledge professionals need to innovate and develop new models for their role and contribution. In other words, information professionals need to innovate in their own organizations, to develop innovation skills and competencies and to reform their role and perceptions of their role, in order to more strongly position themselves to support the wider innovation agenda; we term this 'double-loop' innovation.

Reflect: Do you agree with the following quote: 'Imagination is more important than knowledge' – Albert Einstein (quoted by Heye, 2006, 257)?

Summary and conclusions

This chapter has taken the reader on a journey through a number of aspects of innovation in practice. The first section ventured into a number of aspects of the innovation project. The first stage is the development of ideas and the identification of opportunities, and the difference between an idea and an opportunity was discussed. Opportunities arise from changes in the organizational environment, problems, needs and gaps in the marketplace. Another important aspect of the innovation project is the process of concept testing and development, during which ideas are developed and subjected to evaluation on the basis of their viability. Finally, it is important to consider the implementation phase of innovation, which brings the new service or product to realization. Three other topics have also been considered in this chapter: customer/user involvement in innovation, collaborative and open innovation and the potential for information organizations to facilitate access to information and knowledge to support innovation by other public sector, voluntary and commercial organizations. By engaging customers in innovation processes, organizations can not only benefit from customer knowledge and interest, but can also gain a greater understanding of the way in which customers use a product or service, which, in turn, will enhance design and has the potential to improve adoption and use. In addition, organizations that collaborate with other organizations, or engage in open innovation and innovation networks, can benefit considerably by a mutual exchange of benefits that enhances their capacity to innovate. There are a range of different types of innovation networks, and successful collaboration depends crucially on the management of relationships, processes and resources.

The chapter, and the book, concludes with a section that argues for the wider role of information professionals in innovation in organizations, communities and societies, based in the intimate relationship between knowledge, learning and innovation.

Review questions

1 Discuss the difference between an idea and an opportunity.
2 Evaluate the potential sources of ideas towards innovation.

3 What are the key considerations associated with concept testing and development?

4 What are the key factors that determine innovation project success?

5 Who are lead users, and what are the potential benefits of engaging them in innovation?

6 In what ways can customers be engaged in the co-creation of a service experience?

7 What are the potential benefits of open innovation?

8 Outline, and give examples of, some of the different types of innovation networks.

9 What factors need to be managed to optimize the performance of an innovation network?

10 Explain the role of information and knowledge in innovation.

11 Offer some examples of how information organizations might support innovation processes in other organizations.

Challenges

1 Recognizing an opportunity!

2 Achieving a new service or product that has a sufficient level of product/service viability, industry/market viability, organizational viability and financial viability.

3 Managing the factors that lead to a successful outcome for an innovation project.

4 Evaluating the success of an innovation project.

5 Finding and choosing the 'right' customers and getting their commitment to contribute to your innovation.

6 Understanding how to achieve customer community leadership in specific organizational contexts and industry sectors.

7 Managing the potential tensions in innovation networks in order to optimize their innovation performance.

8 At organizational level, co-ordinating engagement in innovation partnerships and networks, and aligning the potential outcomes from these partnerships with the strategic direction of the organization.

9 For information organizations, building and maintaining reputations that

lead them to be perceived as preferred collaborating organizations.
10 Developing innovative competencies that support information organizations in their role as contributors to innovation in other organizations.

Group discussion topics
Group discussion topic 1: The innovation project
Considering a recent innovation project in which you have been involved:

1 How did you go about generating ideas and opportunities?
2 How did you assess the viability of the potential new service, process or product?
3 What were the particular challenges in innovation?

Group discussion topic 2: Customer/user innovation
1 Does your information organization have lead users who are useful to engage in the innovation process? How do you work with them?
2 What are the challenges and opportunities offered by Web 2.0 and other social networking technologies in the area of innovation?

Group discussion topic 3: Open innovation
Thinking of a recent innovation project that you have undertaken in partnership with other organizations:

1 How many organizations were involved?
2 What were the challenges in working together?
3 What were the benefits of the collaboration?

References and additional reading
Adams, R., Bessant, J. and Phelps, R. (2006) Innovation Management Measurement: a review, *International Journal of Management Reviews*, **8** (1), 21–47.

Amabile, T., Conti, R., Coon, H., Lazenby, J. and Herron, M. (1996) Assessing the Work Environment for Creativity, *Academy of Management Journal*, **39** (5), 1154–84.

Barringer, B. R. and Ireland, R. D. (2008) *Entrepreneurship: successfully launching new ventures*, 2nd edn, Pearson Education International.

Beckman, T. J. (1999) The Current State of Knowledge Management. In Liebowitz, J. (ed.), *Knowledge Management Handbook*, CRC Press.

Bessant, J. and Tidd, J. (2007) *Innovation and Entrepreneurship*, Wiley.

Blackler, F. (1995) Knowledge, Knowledge Work and Organizations: an overview and interpretation, *Organization Studies*, **16** (6), 1021–46.

Bragge, J., Tuunanen, T. and Marttiin, P. (2009) Inviting Lead-users from Virtual Communities to Co-create Innovative IS Services in a Structured Groupware Environment, *Service Science*, **1** (4), 241–55.

Cefai, J. (2010) Let's Go Shopping, *Library + Information Gazette*, 14–27 January, 8.

Chapman, R. L. and Corso, M. (2005) From Continuous Improvement to Collaborative Innovation: the next challenge in supply chain management, *Production Planning & Control*, **16** (4), 339–44.

Chen, C-J. (2004) The Effects of Knowledge Attributes, Alliance Characteristics, and Absorptive Capacity on Knowledge Transfer Performance, *R&D Management*, **34** (3), 311–21.

Cohen, W. M. and Levinthal, D. A. (1990) Absorptive Capacity: a new perspective on learning and innovation, *Administrative Science Quarterly*, **35**, 128–52.

Coleman, D. (1999) Groupware: collaboration and knowledge sharing. In Liebowitz, J. (ed.), *Knowledge Management Handbook*, CRC Press.

Colombo, M. G., Rabbiosi, L. and Reichstein, T. (2010) Designing Internal Organization for External Knowledge Sourcing,

European Management Review, **7** (1), 74–6.

Coulson-Thomas, C. (2004) The Knowledge Entrepreneurship Challenge: moving on from knowledge sharing to knowledge creation and exploitation, *The Learning Organization*, **11** (1), 84–93.

Cullen, J. (2007) Information Work and the Opportunity of Innovation: from corporate to social product development, *Business Information Review*, **24** (3), 156–60.

Dahlsten, F. (2004) Hollywood Wives Revisited: a study of customer involvement in the XC90 project at Volvo Cars, *European Journal of Management*, **7** (2), 141–9.

Darroch, J. and McNaughton, R. (2002) Examining the Link between Knowledge Management Practices and Types of Innovation, *Journal of Intellectual Capital*, **3** (3), 210–22.

Dasgupta, M. and Gupta, R. K. (2009) Innovation in Organizations: a review of the role of organizational learning and knowledge management, *Global Business Review*, **10** (2), 213–24.

Davenport, T. H., De Long, D. W. and Beers, M. C. (1998) Successful Knowledge Management Projects, *Sloan Management Review*, **39** (2), 43–57.

Desouza, K. C. et al. (2008) Customer-driven Innovation, *Research-Technology Management*, **51** (3), 35–44.

Du Chatenier, E., Verstegen, J. A. A. M., Biemand, H. J. A., Mulder, M. and Omta, O. (2009) The Challenges of Collaborative Knowledge Creation in Open Innovation Teams, *Human Resource Development Review*, **8** (3), 350–81.

Du Plessis, M. (2007) The Role of Knowledge Management in Innovation, *Journal of Knowledge Management*, **11** (4), 20–9.

Gibbert, M., Leibold, M. and Probst, G. (2002) Five Styles of Customer Knowledge Management, and How Smart Companies Use Them to Create Value, *European Management Journal*, **20** (5), 459–69.

Gloet, M. and Terziovski, M. (2004) Exploring the Relationship between Knowledge Management Practice and Innovation

Performance, *Journal of Manufacturing Technology Management*, **15** (5), 402–9.

Heye, D. (2006) Creativity and Innovation: two key characteristics of the successful 21st century information professional, *Business Information Review*, **23** (4), 252–7.

Hsieh, L. F. and Chen, S. K. (2005) Incorporating Voice of the Consumer: does it really work?, *Industrial Management & Data Systems*, **105** (5/6), 769–85.

Hull, R., Coombs, R. and Peltu, M. (2000) Knowledge Management Practices for Innovation: an audit tool for improvement, *International Journal of Technology Management*, **20** (5–8), 633–56.

Jones, R. and Rowley, J. (2010) Networks and Customer Relationships in a Small Software Technology Firm: a case study, *Journal of Small Business Enterprise*, forthcoming.

Ketchen, D. I., Ireland, D. R. and Snow, C. C. (2007) Strategic Entrepreneurship, Collaborative Innovation, and Wealth Creation, *Strategic Entrepreneurship Journal*, **1** (3–4), 317–85.

Kristensson, P., Gustafsson, A. and Archer, T. (2004) Harnessing the Creative Potential among Users, *Journal of Product Innovation Management*, **21** (1), 4–14.

Li, L. (2009) *Emerging Technologies for Academic Librarians in the Digital Age*, Chandos.

Li, X. (2006) Library as Incubating Space for Innovations: practice, trends and skill sets, *Library Management*, **27** (6/7), 370–8.

Light, P. C. (1998) *Sustaining Innovation: creating nonprofit and government organizations that innovate naturally*, Jossey-Bass.

Matthing, J., Sanden, B. and Edvardsson, B. (2004) New Service Development: learning from and with customers, *International Journal of Service Industry Management*, **15** (5), 479–98.

Miles, R. E., Miles, G. and Snow, C. C. (2005) *Collaborative Entrepreneurship: how communities of networked firms use continuous innovation to create economic wealth*, Stanford University Press.

Morrison, P. D., Roberts, J. H. and Von Hippel, E. (2000) Determinants of User Innovation Sharing in a Local Market, *Management Science*, **46** (12), 1513–27.

Nambisan, S. (2002) Designing Virtual Customer Environments for New Product Development: toward a theory, *Academy of Management Review*, **27** (3), 392–413.

National Library of Scotland (2004) *Policy Documents: submission to Cultural Commission by the National Library of Scotland*, www.nls.uk.

Nijboer, J. (2006) Cultural Entrepreneurship in Libraries, *New Library World*, **107** (9–10), 434–43.

Nonaka, I. (1991) The Knowledge-creating Company, *Harvard Business Review*, November–December, 96–104.

Payne, A. E., Storbacka, K. and Frow, P. (2008) Managing the Co-creation of Value, *Journal of the Academy of Marketing Science*, **36** (1), 83–96.

Prahalad, C. K. and Ramaswamy, V. (2000) Co-opting Customer Competence, *Harvard Business Review*, **78** (1), 79–81.

Rae, D. (2007) *Entrepreneurship: from opportunity to action*, Palgrave Macmillan.

Rowley, J., Kupiec-Teahan, B. and Leeming, E. (2007) Customer Community and Co-creation: a case study, *Marketing Intelligence and Planning*, **25** (2), 136–46.

Sawhney, M., Verona, G. and Prandelli, E. (2005) Collaborating to Create: the internet as a platform for customer engagement in product innovation, *Journal of Interactive Marketing*, **19** (4), 4–17.

Sonderquist, K., Chanaron, J. and Motwani, J. (1997) Managing Innovation in French Small and Medium Sized Enterprises: an empirical study, *Benchmarking for Quality Management and Technology*, **4** (4), 259–72.

Swink, M. (2006) Building Collaborative Innovation Capability, *Research Technology Management*, March–April, 37–47.

Tang, H. K. (1999) An Inventory of Organizational Innovativeness, *Technovation*, **19** (1), 41–51.

Von Hippel, E. (1986) Lead Users: a source of novel product concepts, *Management Science*, **32** (7), 791–805.

Von Hippel, E. (2005) *Democratizing Innovation*, MIT Press.

Von Krogh, G. (1998) Care in Knowledge Creation, *California Management Review*, **40**, 133–53.

Wallis, R. (2009) Setting Innovation Loose with 'Juice', *Library + Information Gazette*, 22 October, 5.

Wenger, E. (2000) Communities of Practice and Social Learning Systems, *Organization*, **7** (2), 225–46.

Woodward, H. and Estelle, L. (2009) Why Research Needs Order, Not Anarchy, in Cyberspace, *Library & Information Update*, November, 32–3.

Index